SELLING CRUISES

Second Edition

Join us on the web at

hospitality-tourism.delmar.com

SELLING CRUISES

Second Edition

Claudine Dervaes

THOMSON

DELMAR LEARNING

Australia Canada Mexico Singapore Spain United Kingdom United States

THOMSON

DELMAR LEARNING

Selling Cruises, 2nd edition
Claudine Dervaes

Business Unit Director:
Susan L. Simpfenderfer

Senior Acquisitions Editor:
Joan M. Gill

Editorial Assistant:
Lisa Flatley

Executive Production Manager:
Wendy A. Troeger

Production Manager:
Carolyn Miller

Production Editor:
Kathryn B. Kucharek

Executive Marketing Manager:
Donna J. Lewis

Channel Manager:
Wendy E. Mapstone

Cover Image:
PhotoDisc/Getty Images

For permission to use material from this text or product, contact us by
Tel   (800) 730-2214
Fax   (800) 730-2215
http://www.thomsonrights.com

Library of Congress Cataloging-in-Publication Data
Dervaes, Claudine.
  Selling cruises / Caludine Dervaes.—2nd ed.
    p. cm.
  ISBN 0-7668-4947-3
  1. Ocean travel.   2. Cruise ships.   I. Title.
  G550 .D46 2002
  910.4'5—dc21   2002025969

NOTICE TO THE READER

Contents

Introduction and How to Use This Manual

This manual is designed to be both a training tool and a reference tool. As such, it contains both text and exercises to ensure retention of the material.

Because the cruise industry changes continually, the user is advised to update the information as necessary.

A current, thorough atlas is suggested as a complement to this manual. Cruise line brochures and other references are also helpful.

This manual is part of The Travel Training Series set of manuals—the other sections include *Travel Geography, Domestic Travel and Ticketing, Selling Tours and Independent Travel, International Travel,* and *Sales and Marketing Techniques. The Travel Dictionary* is another resource for all the terms, codes, and abbreviations used in travel.

HOW TO USE THIS MANUAL

Read and complete the exercises provided. Do as much outside research as possible, using references and resources that are listed. Make notes on applicable pages when changes or updates are obtained from industry sources. Once this manual is completed, it can serve as a valuable desk reference and sales tool.

Attention: Teachers

The answers to the questions are available on the Internet at www.hospitality-tourism.delmar.com when you click on Resources. It is suggested that instructors purchase a copy of *Teaching Travel: A Handbook for the Educator.* It provides lesson plans, games for the classroom, projects, teaching hints and techniques, useful forms, and much more.

What's different about this edition? Although we have tried to provide the same information as in previous editions, this manual has had to be updated in many areas. Therefore, we suggest instructors review the entire manual to familiarize themselves with changed and added information.

CHAPTER 1

Introduction to Cruises

HIGHLIGHTS OF THIS CHAPTER INCLUDE:

- ✦ Industry Reference Books and Resources
- ✦ Types of Cruises
- ✦ Cruise Details
- ✦ Food and Drink
- ✦ Questions and Answers About Cruises
- ✦ The Cruise Vacation!
- ✦ Cruise Industry Trends and Changes

A cruise can be a wonderful experience, and there are many types of cruise lines, cruise ships, itineraries, and amenities. There are also many areas of the world to cruise. Cruises include day trips to "nowhere," transatlantic voyages, three- or four-night cruises to the Bahamas, five- to seven-day cruises to the Caribbean, cruises on the Nile, through the Panama Canal, or around the world. There are also freighter trips, port-to-port and ferry services, and local cruises. Generally, cruises offer the feeling of getting away from it all, a feeling of glamour, prestige, and romance. They can also be learning experiences, or a great way to celebrate family reunions, marriages, anniversaries, and graduations. And don't forget that conferences, seminars, and business meetings can be held on a cruise ship. Cruise travel can also be used as an incentive (as a reward for employee performance). The great part is that the cruise price includes accommodations, meals, entertainment (movies, shows, nightclubs, discos, etc.), shipboard sports and recreational facilities, and stops at ports of call. Unpack only once and enjoy all the activities. Make friends and feel pampered. The meals on board most cruises provide fine dining experiences—with a variety of superb salads, soups, entrées, and desserts or exquisite buffets.

There are many reference books, guidebooks, magazines, and videos about cruises. There are also software programs and on-line services providing information about cruises, availability, and reservations.

NOTES ON USING REFERENCES AND RESOURCES

Make sure to obtain current copies of references—information changes continually. Make changes to the information in this manual as necessary.

There are advantages and disadvantages to the different references and it's important for the travel professional to have *both* consumer references and industry references to access all the information.

Contact bookstores, libraries, the Internet, or Delmar Learning for current ordering information.

Staff experiences are also very important. Besides familiarization or "fam trip" opportunities allowing agents to sail at reduced rates, there are various seminars and conferences on board the ships that provide ways to learn about specific ships, destinations, sales, and marketing skills. Site inspections of other ships may also be possible.

Finding the right cruise for clients requires imagination, research, listening skills, and restraint from jumping at price alone. The most important aspects will involve determining the clients' interests and lifestyle, plus their needs and expectations. More details will be covered in the chapter on selecting, selling, and pricing cruises.

Cruises appeal to many types and ages of people. There is hardly an average cruise passenger when so many factors are involved. Items that influence the type of passenger include the cruise line, the particular ship, time of year, itinerary, length of cruise, and cost of cruise. For example, a three-night cruise to the Bahamas in late May or early June might have high school students as average passengers, since that is a popular time for senior trips and graduation celebrations. Sometimes there are "theme" cruises, featuring a particular interest, such as astronomy, music, or sports, which can attract certain types of passengers. Some cruises have guest lecturers on a variety of topics or special guest performers. And there are cruises that include activities for special occasions (Thanksgiving, Christmas, New Year's Day, etc.).

The cruise industry has expanded dramatically and continues to grow, with new cruise lines, new and different types of ships, changing itineraries—all offering different cruise traveler experiences.

INDUSTRY REFERENCE BOOKS AND RESOURCES

Official Cruise Guide—Annual publication by the Northstar Travel Media, P.O. Box 10706, Riverton, NJ 08076-5117. Cost is approximately $85.00. This guide contains extensive information and is generally an industry reference rather than a consumer resource. The OCG (as it is abbreviated) includes charts and information on ships, plus a "clientele profile," which is quite valuable when recommending cruises. It gives percentages of types of passengers (singles, couples under age 35, couples age 35–45, couples over age 55, and sometimes includes the passengers' nationality—American, Canadian, European, etc.). Northstar Travel Media also produces The *STAR SERVICE,* an objective guide to hotels and cruises. Star Service has a Web site <http://www.starserviceonline.com.> Call (877) 902-9757 for subscription details.

Official Steamship Guide International—Published four times a year, 9111 Cross Park Drive, Suite D247, Knoxville, TN 37923. (800) 783-4903, Fax (423) 694-0848. This is another industry publication that is used by most travel agents for obtaining sailing dates and ship itineraries, plus other information.

Worldwide Publishing Services offers the *Official Cruise Rates and Dates* and *Worldwide Ferry Services* manuals. Contact Edward Catalozzi, POB 40819, Providence, RI 02940. (508) 252-9896, <http://www.cruiseferry.com>. e-mail: cruiseferry@cs.com.

CLIA—The Cruise Lines International Association publishes a manual for travel agents, and has pamphlets, training videos, and other items. CLIA also offers training academies and certification programs. CLIA's Cruise Counselor Certification Program offers two achievement levels: ACC (accredited cruise counselor) and MCC (master cruise counselor). Enroll by contacting CLIA, 500 Fifth Avenue, Suite 1407, New York, NY 10110. (212) 921-0066. Fax (212) 921-0549. Web site <http://www.cruising.org>.

Cruise Line Brochures, Cruise Videos—These are the working tools of travel agents in selling and promoting cruises. They are ordered from the various cruise lines or distribution companies. Current copies should be on file at all times. Agents sometimes create their own customized copies of brochures, highlighting the important areas and specific passenger information.

Software and On-line Information—The CRSs (Computer Reservation Systems)/GDSs (Global Distribution Systems) in travel agencies have on-line information/booking capabilities. Consult the agency's training manual for assistance. Searches on the Internet will list thousands of sites for information. Web site addresses are given in the listing section of this manual.

Other References Available Through Many Bookstores:

Note: Prices subject to change.

Berlitz Complete Guide to Cruising—$21.95. This statistical, concise reference includes useful details such as passenger space ratios (achieved by dividing the gross registered tonnage by the passenger capacity), and lists of ratings on ship appearance/condition, cleanliness, comfort, entertainment, cabin service, decor, fitness and other facilities, value for money, and total cruise experience. Particularly useful are the "comments" paragraphs at the end of each ship listing, summarizing the ship.

Stern's Guide to the Cruise Vacation—$17.95. This book provides details on the ports of call and has many photographs of ships, decks and interiors, sample menus, and activity programs. Interestingly, there are two chapters on "cruising for joggers" and "cruising for tennis buffs," providing details on those sports at the various ports of call.

Frommer's Guide to Cruises—$19.00. This reference combines the reviews of ships with paragraphs of descriptions—no charts, lists, or specifications. A notable feature is that at the beginning of the cruise line information it states the cruising grounds and itineraries of the different ships. Unfortunately, that information can change. The paragraphs about the ships predominantly cover two subjects: cabins and public rooms, although at times an "activities" category is included.

Fielding's Guide to Worldwide Cruises—$17.95. An excellent reference, containing extensive information on ships, ports of call, and cruise regions and ships available. It provides the history of the different cruise lines and ships and also has numerous "author's tips," which are very helpful.

Fodor's Cruises and Ports Of Call—$18.00. Similar in thoroughness to *Fielding's*, *Fodor's* combines a general profile of the cruise line followed by reviews of ships. Information is categorized in a paragraph about the fleet, followed by the "cruise experience," which has subcategories of activities, dining, entertainment, service and tipping, destinations, and so on. Details include cabin and rate charts, facilities, specifications, and a "ship's log," which has summary-type information.

And More! A search done through <http://www.amazon.com.> produced over 100 results. However, many publications had old copyright dates, making them ineffective for today's marketplace and current cruise knowledge and skills. Some were very specific in their content, focusing on cruising areas, ports of call, bargain hunting, and the like. Here are a few other recommendations for complete guides: *THE UNOFFICIAL GUIDE TO CRUISES*—$17.95, *THE COMPLETE IDIOT'S GUIDE TO CRUISE VACATIONS*—$16.95, *CRUISE VACATIONS FOR DUMMIES*—$17.95.

Magazines

Trade Magazine Supplements—Publications such as *Travel Weekly, Travel Trade, Travel Age,* and *Travel Agent* periodically offer special issues on cruise industry news. Contact your travel agency, visit the public library, or consult *The Travel Dictionary* for subscription contact information.

Cruise Travel—Published by Century World Publishing, P.O. Box 342, Mt. Morris, IL 61054. (800) 877-5893. <http://www.cruisetravelmag.com> Subscriptions are approximately $12.00 a year. You may also see copies at newsstands or bookstores.

Porthole—Published six times a year. For subscription requests, contact Porthole, P.O. Box 469066, Escondido, CA 92046-9066. (800) 776-7678, <http://www.porthole.com>.

Newsletters

Millergram—Published quarterly, this newsletter relates cruise industry news with short bits on new ships, shipbuilding contracts, itinerary changes, and more. Contact Bill Miller Cruises Everywhere, P.O. Box 1643, Secaucus, NJ 07096. (201) 348-9390. $10.00 a year.

Ocean and Cruise News—Published monthly, this newsletter reviews a different ship each month and also reports on itinerary changes and discounted sailings. Contact the World Ocean and Cruise Liner Society, Box 92-B, Stamford, CT 06904. (203) 329-2787 (phone and fax), <http://www.ocean-cruisenews.com>. $30.00 a year.

Travltips—This newsletter guide to freighter travel is available by contacting Travltips, P.O. Box 580188, Flushing, NY 11358. (800) 872-8584, (718) 939-2400, Fax (718) 939-2047, <http://www.travltips.com>.

CruiseReports—Unbiased cruise ship ratings based on the consensus/judgment of passengers, 25 Washington Street, Morristown, NJ 07960. (973) 605-2442, <http://www.cruise-report.com>. 12 issues, about $70.00 a year.

Electronic newsletter available free (eCruiseNews) from the World's Leading Cruise Lines. Contact <http://www.leaderships.com>.

Other Resources

How to Get a Job with a Cruise Line, by Mary Fallon Miller. This insider's guide to the jobs on board cruise ships is available in many bookstores. $16.95.

THE INTERNET

The Web sites of the individual cruise lines are provided in the list of cruise lines and ships later on in this manual. There are other Web sites to check for information and booking cruises. Here are just a few:

<http://www.Expedia.com>

<http://www.Travelocity.com>

<http://www.CruisePath.net> (offers CruiseManager developed by GoCruiseDirect.com)

<http://www.justcruises.com>

<http://www.cybercruises.com>

<http://www.cruise411.com>

<http://www.smallshipcruises.com>

<http://www.cruisesonly.com>—part of www.mytravelco.com>

<http://www.CruiseMates.com>

<http://www.CruiseGal.com>

<http://www.Cruises-n-More.com>

<http://www.11thhourvacations.com>

<http://www.cruisestar.com>

<http://www.i-cruise.com>

<http://www.thecruisemarketplace.com>

<http://www.cruise2.com>

<http://www.moments-notice.com>

<http://www.cruise.com>

TYPES OF CRUISES

Some cruise lines fall into a certain category and some have ships that fit into each of the categories. Particular cruise lines and ships will be covered later.

Mass Market Cruises

These cruises appeal to the mass market, and are budget to moderately priced. They often feature the Bahamas, the Caribbean, Bermuda, or Alaska as destinations.

Upscale Cruises

These cruises appeal to more experienced cruisers. These passengers have more money to spend, want first-class service, and are looking for new ports of call and destinations.

Luxury Cruises

These cruises offer elegance, ultra-modern style, numerous amenities, and unique itineraries—at prices that only the wealthy can afford.

Specialty Cruises

A wide range of specialty cruises are available, including whale watching, diving, barge cruises, sailing ships, and exploratory voyages.

Local Cruises

A different type of "cruise" may be available at destinations for local sightseeing or entertainment. Some cities, resort areas, and destinations offer sightseeing, dinner, and specialty cruises. These local cruises are sometimes included on packages and tours or are sold locally through hotel desks or tourist bureaus. These are cruises of short duration, involving an optional local activity, and may utilize a gondola, fishing boat, sailboat, trimaran or catamaran, steamboat, or small cruise ship. It may be a sightseeing cruise, a lunch trip, a chance for fishing or shelling, a dinner/dance cruise, or a gambling opportunity. It may go down a river, a coastal waterway, offshore, or to nearby islands.

CHAPTER 1, REVIEW 1

1. Name three references for information on cruises. _____
   _____

2. Although the average cruise passenger might be age 40 to 50, state three factors that influence the type of passengers. _____
   _____

3. Other than a vacation, what are three other reasons for taking a cruise? _____
   _____

4. Four main types of cruises are *mass market, upscale, luxury,* and _____
   _____

5. Name four possible "themes" that cruises might feature. _____
   _____

CRUISE DETAILS

Length of Cruises

There are one-day cruises to nowhere; two-, three-, four-, five-, seven-, ten-, and 14-day cruises; and around-the-world cruises that take about 90 days.

Air/Sea Programs

Cruise prices often include or offer coordinated airfare from many cities to the port of embarkation. Some cruise lines organize round-trip air charters from major cities to the port. If clients don't use the airfare provided, there is usually an air credit amount offered. Cruise lines also offer special add-on packages and features for stays prior to or after the cruise. It's important to check if the air/sea rate is better or worse than using an available excursion fare. Also, flights booked by the cruise lines for the air/sea programs may be less desirable and convenient. With some lines, passengers can pay extra for air deviation privileges, such as requesting a non-stop flight (if there is one). More details on air/sea programs are provided later in this manual.

Location and Types of Cabins

Some ships today have all outside cabins (cabins with portholes). Others have outside and inside cabins. Inside cabins are normally less expensive. Generally, staterooms or cabins are smaller than comparable hotel rooms. Cabins can have twin beds, double/queen beds, or upper and lower beds (like bunk beds). Suites and deluxe cabin accommodations have sitting rooms in addition to the sleeping room. Some cabins have just a shower; others may have a bath or both. Luxury ships offer hair dryers, mini-bars, and in-room safes. Other amenities, such as phones, radios, TVs, and VCRs, plus data ports for computers, may be provided. Balconies have become very popular, and new ships often have a majority of cabins with this feature.

Number of People per Cabin

Some cabins accommodate only two people, others accommodate up to four. Some ships have connecting cabins to handle more than four. Cruise prices are normally stated "per person, double occupancy" (PPDO) and then offer a "third/fourth person" rate. For example, a cabin rate of $1,195.00 PPDO and a third/fourth person rate of $625.00 would cost a total of $3,640.00 if four people occupy the cabin ($910.00 each). If a single person occupies the cabin, a 50% to 100% supplement is usually charged (if the cabin rate is $1,195.00, single occupancy at a 50% supplement would cost $1,792.50). However, some ships offer a "share basis" rate (a cabin mate may be assigned) or a "guaranteed single" rate, where the single passenger will be assigned a cabin at time of departure. Cruise lines may waive the single supplement for cruises not fully booked to encourage business. More details on pricing a cruise will be covered later.

Services

Passengers will feel pampered as the stewards efficiently clean the staterooms while passengers are at breakfast or out and about. Stewards turn down the beds in the evening, usually leaving mints or chocolates on pillows. Restaurant stewards and bus persons service passengers while dining. Other personnel include the maître d', wine steward(s), bartenders, lounge staff, deck staff, and purser's office staff (for mail, banking services, problems, and questions). The cruise director is like a cruise ship host/hostess. The director is responsible for all social activities on board and should be very visible and available to the passengers. Depending on the ship, the duties of the director include giving lectures, calling bingo, introducing entertainers, and maybe performing in the shows. Cruise directors have assistants who help ensure the passengers enjoy the voyage. There are staff members who supervise the children's and teens' activities and programs. Virtually every ship has fully equipped medical facilities and staff to handle emergencies. There is usually a chapel for non-denominational services. Laundry services may be available and some cruises provide dry cleaning (there are additional charges for these services, unless passengers are using a self-service launderette).

Entertainment

Cruises usually offer variety shows, bingo, deck areas and pools, spas, games, a library, sports activities, contests, movies, lectures, and more. There are lounges with entertainment and dancing areas/discos/karaoke. Movies may be available in a theater on board or through the TVs in the cabins. Supervised activities for children and teens are provided. Tours of the galley (ship's kitchen) and bridge (the captain's work area) may be offered. And these are all included in the cruise price. Rock climbing, ice-skating, more unique activities, and Internet rooms are offered on some ships. There are usually additional charges for these activities. Meeting rooms are available on most ships for conferences or group parties/events. More on group travel is provided in the final chapter.

Space and Passenger to Crew Ratios

The *passenger space ratio* is determined by dividing the gross registered tonnage of a ship (a measure of size) by the regular passenger capacity of the ship. Luxury ships will generally have a space ratio of at least 35 to 40 cubic feet. However, the space ratio measurement can be misleading since the regular capacity does not account for third and fourth passengers and because of what is included in the ship's space (galley, crew quarters, engine room, etc.). A standard method of comparing services of ships is to examine the ratio between the number of passengers and the number of crew. Luxury ships will often feature this ratio—such as one crewmember for every one or two passengers—implying the specialized attention given to the passengers.

More About the Passengers

There is no typical cruise passenger. People who take cruises come from all walks of life, backgrounds, and cultures. What's special about cruise passengers is that they develop a sense of "belonging," as that particular group is together on that ship on the specific cruise. They develop a sense of camaraderie. People are generally inclined to make friends on cruises. They have things in common to talk about—the food, the entertainment, the cabins, everything! The organized activities bring people together, and the contests and events highlight certain passengers (the man who won the "hairy chest" contest!).

FOOD AND DRINK

Most cruises feature lavish buffets, extensive menus, and regular and specialty drinks. Meals are included in the cruise price; drinks are priced similarly to bar prices or included on some cruises. Some lines offer a card for unlimited sodas, such as Carnival Cruise Line's "Fountain Fun Card," which presently costs $14.95 for three-day cruises and $29.95 for seven-day voyages. The dining rooms feature a variety of entrées, plus appetizers, soups, salads, breads, and desserts. The food is one of the best features of cruises, as there is virtually no limit on what or how much you can order. And, in most cases, the entrées are gourmet and special. Duty-free liquor can be purchased on board. In some cases, ships restrict passengers from consuming on board purchases of duty-free liquor, requiring that the purchases be delivered at the end of the cruise. Special diets may be available. Passengers usually choose a meal "sitting" at the time of reservation. Example times are:

> First Sitting—Breakfast 7:30 A.M., Lunch 12:00 P.M., Dinner 6:00 P.M.
>
> Late/Second Sitting—Breakfast 8:30 A.M., Lunch 1:00 P.M., Dinner 8:00 P.M.

The doors to dining rooms may close 15 minutes after the assigned time so that all the courses may be served efficiently. Dining areas primarily feature tables for six/eight, with some tables for four and maybe a few for two. The room may be non-smoking or have non-smoking areas. Check with the cruise line to reserve a special type of table. On some ships table assignments are made at the port on a first come, first served basis. Passengers are usually expected to sit at the same table for all meals during the cruise. Dining times are when you get to know the passengers assigned to your table. The waiter and bus person try to learn your likes and dislikes, and to be efficient at remembering specifics (prefer tea, not coffee, like lots of water, vegetarian entrées, etc.). If you don't like your tablemates, speak with the maître d'. Sometimes dining is on an open seating basis, where tables are not assigned. If there is a problem with a table assignment, contact the maître d' or the purser.

In addition to breakfast, lunch, and dinner, most ships have an "early risers coffee and rolls," mid-morning tea and coffee, afternoon tea, and midnight buffets with lavish food displays. Soft drinks, snacks, and cocktails may also be available for delivery to cabins around the clock. Some cruise lines offer restaurant alternatives, such as pizza parlors, icecream parlors, and outdoor barbeques. Some cruises will feature theme-dining nights, such as "Italian night"—with special menus and decorations. Most cruises have a "Captain's Party" night and a "Farewell Dinner," which are usually more formal affairs.

NEW DINING INNOVATIONS—On some ships there are "restaurants" rather than dining rooms. And certain cruise lines have changed the traditional sitting arrangements.

- Norwegian Cruise Line (NCL) introduced "freestyle" cruising with dining options that include choice of restaurants, times, dining partners, and attire preferences. New activities such as Internet access and health and wellness programs have been introduced. The disembarkation process has also been changed to a leisurely format on NCL. Carnival Cruise Line and Princess Cruise Line have also begun offering flexible dining choices. These programs include extended dining hours and varied dining styles.

- Carnival Cruise Lines introduced "Total Choice Dining," featuring four staggered seating times in main restaurants, the launch of dining room "Team Service," and enhancements to its Seaview Bistros, the line's casual dinner-time alternative restaurants. In the main restaurants, guests are assigned to one of four seating times: 6:00 P.M., 6:45 P.M., 8:00 P.M., and 8:45 P.M. Team Service enables wait staff to be more attentive to passengers because of an increase in the number of personnel serving each table.

- Princess Cruises unveiled "personal choice dining," which is like Norwegian Cruise Line's "freestyle" with a twist. Passengers choose flexible dining or assigned seating (which will continue in at least one dining room per ship). The choice must be made when booking.

SAMPLE DINNER MENU

Hors d'oeuvres: Veal salad   Champignons in oil
Stuffed olives   Sausages in sauce

Soups: Hot consommé   Italian vegetable   Clam chowder

Entrées: Pot roast of beef, Neapolitan style
Breaded veal Milanese
Broiled red snapper, Cajun style
Pasta with meat sauce and sausage
Vegetables with rice and a butter wine sauce

Vegetables: Creamed turnips   Buttered peas   French fries
Broccoli   Baked potato

Sauces: Mint   Apple   Tartar   Mayonnaise

Salads: Cucumber   Tomato   Lettuce   Spinach

Dressings: French   Italian   Thousand island   Roquefort

Desserts: Icecreams (vanilla, chocolate, pistachio)
Strawberry pie   German chocolate cake   Assorted pastries
Fresh fruit assortment   Assorted cheeses

Beverages: Coffee (regular and decaf)   Tea (hot and iced)

Silverware Survival Tips

For those who choose the luxury of the formal dining rooms for meals, an incomparable experience awaits! Don't be intimidated by the number of utensils. In a standard formal place setting, there are two forks to the left of the plate, a knife and two spoons to the right. Above the forks is the bread and butter plate with the butter knife (small handle, flat blade) lying across the upper edge of the plate. A fork and a spoon are above the plate. You can identify silverware by its placement and appearance. At the far left is the salad fork (shorter handle and tines). To the right of the salad fork is the entrée fork. To the right of the dinner plate is the entrée knife (used for salad or entrée). To the right of the knife is a teaspoon (used for a variety of selections) and to the far right is the soup spoon (round-shaped bowl). The fork and spoon above the plate are used for desserts. Glasses are placed in a row above the knife and spoons and are organized by position: from left to right they are water, red wine, and white wine. Use silverware from the outside in and continue working toward the plate with each course. Other implements may be provided by the waitperson (such as a serrated knife for steaks, special utensils used just for snails, crab, etc.). When you lay down your utensils, keep the silverware entirely on the plate. If you want to rest or speak, lay your fork (tines down) and knife crossed in the middle of the plate; and when you are finished, place the knife and fork on the rim of the plate parallel to each other, facing 10 o'clock. Note, however, these are guidelines, not rules etched in stone!

Smoking

Most dining areas are completely non-smoking or have separated areas. Non-smoking areas have expanded to include show lounges on several ships and certain deck eating areas. At the present time there is one completely non-smoking cruise ship.

Carnival's *Paradise*—The Non-Smoking Ship

Carnival Cruise Line initiated the non-smoking ship called the *Paradise* in December 1998. It has been very successful. Passengers sign an agreement at the beginning of the cruise. If a passenger is found with cigarettes or any smoking materials, a $250.00 fine applies and the passenger is removed at the next port of call. Getting back home is at the passenger's expense.

Social Life and Customary Dress

Lounges, cocktail bars, discos, casinos, and other public areas are gathering places for meeting and socializing. Dress is usually very casual on most ships, although some cruise lines and passengers opt for more formal attire. Most ships request that passengers not wear bathing suits in dining rooms. Preferred dress for special parties or events is usually stated in the daily activities program. Evening dress falls into three categories: elegantly casual, informal, and formal. Elegantly casual is comfortable, relaxed clothing (no T-shirts or jeans). Informal dress means dresses and pantsuits for women and lightweight jackets for men (tie optional). Formal evenings mean cocktail dresses or gowns for women and business suits/tuxedos for men. Here is an outline for some cruises:

Length of Cruise	Formal Evenings
2–4 days	1
5–7 days	2
8–11 days	3
12–14 days	4
15–18 days	5
19–21 days	6

The trend, however, is for more casual wear, so you will find cruises that require no jackets or ties the entire time. Some cruises feature special singles activities. Some cruises (usually those longer than four days) feature a costume contest and some passengers will bring an outfit for it. Policies concerning the allowance of the crew to mingle with passengers vary. On some ships the officers are encouraged to dance and talk with passengers, while on other ships they are not.

Types of Passengers

Generally, longer cruises attract older passengers who have more time and money. However, with the changes in market conditions and in the category of one-week to 10-day cruises, a great majority of cruise clients are under age 35. Specific sailings may feature certain groups; for example, in May and June some ships may be inundated with students on graduation trips. There will be more families on cruises during the summer and at holidays because of school vacations. During the winter months, tourists choose cruises to get away from the winter cold/snow. Certain itineraries will attract different types of cruise passengers.

Shore Excursions

As cruises call at ports and destinations, there may be local tours, dive trips, or sightseeing excursions offered by the cruise line. Some cruises offer a package of shore excursions that is purchased prior to the cruise. Shore excursions/tours are purchased on board ship through a form provided to the passengers or through a tour desk/purser's office. More information from A to Z and detailed tips are provided in the following chapter.

Tipping

Certain cruise lines don't require tipping the service crew. Check the brochure or contact the cruise line for this information. Here are some tipping guidelines.

Some cruise lines recommend $8.00 to $10.00 per day per person. This is to be divided among the cabin steward, restaurant steward, and busboy. The tip is usually placed in an envelope and left in the cabin at the end of the cruise. The amount should be in cash (bills, not coins). If you have used the services of the crew extensively, you should compensate accordingly.

Other cruises indicate the following separate amounts:

Cabin Steward/Stateroom Attendant–$3.00–$3.50 a day per person

Restaurant Steward/Waiter–$3.00–$3.50 a day per person

Busboy–$1.50–$2.00 a day per person

Maître d'–If there are section maître d's or restaurant managers (assigned to supervise a number of waiters) guidelines are two to four-night cruise $2.00–$3.00 per person, seven-night cruise $5.00 per person, fourteen-night cruise $10.00 per person. If a maître d' has been particularly helpful, extra may be awarded.

Other personnel may require tips, such as the chief housekeeper, deck staff, the wine steward, and bar staff–15% to 20% of the tab. Suite accommodations sometimes include a butler, who may need to be tipped.

Charges On Board

Many cruise lines issue a card identifying you as a passenger, along with such information as your cabin number, meal sitting, and table number. Information regarding a credit card to be used for payment of charges is also formatted to the card, so all the on board purchases are totaled. At the end of the cruise they are charged to that particular credit card. If you wish to pay for all the on board charges by a different method, check with the cruise line. Many will *not* accept checks; and some do *not* accept cash.

Facilities of the Ships

Ships vary as to the luxury and extent of facilities, but most have at least one pool, a theater, a casino, sauna, gym, medical facility, bars and lounges, nightclub, kids' playroom, shops, dining rooms, a beauty parlor, plus promenade and sun decks, a library, game room, and more. There may also be a basketball court, ping-pong tables, putting green, shuffleboard, and other special facilities. Royal Caribbean Cruise Line's *Voyager of the Seas* has a rock-climbing wall, an ice rink, an inline skating track, a golf-simulator, and a nine-hole putting green. Cabins can feature extras such as bathtubs (most have showers only), verandahs, or a lounge area. Stateroom doors may have peepholes for security.

These are just a few of the details of cruises. More information is provided in the next chapter, particularly the list of specifics in "Cruise Specifics from A to Z."

CHAPTER 1, REVIEW 2

1. Inside cabins are usually (more/less) _____ expensive than outside cabins.

2. A single passenger may pay a 50% to 100% supplement. However, some ships offer a "share basis" rate. What does that mean? _____

_____

3. How is the passenger space ratio determined? _____

_____

4. What kinds of passengers may be on a May or June sailing? _____

_____

5. Name eight facilities found on most cruise ships. _____

_____

6. The cabin steward is usually tipped $_____ to $_____ a day per person.

7. The waiter is usually tipped $_____ to $_____ a day per person.

8. The busboy is normally tipped $_____ per person per day.

9. What are the cruise director's usual responsibilities? _____

_____

10. A standard way of comparing services of ships is to examine the ratio between the number of passengers and _____.

11. What does Norwegian Cruise Line's new "freestyle" cruising encompass? _____

_____

12. Give sample times for the first sitting for meals: Breakfast_____ Lunch_____ Dinner_____

13. At open seating meals tables are not assigned. True or False. _____

14. If there is a problem with the table assignment or sitting, passengers should contact the _____ or _____.

15. What is the name of Carnival Cruise Line's non-smoking ship? _____

QUESTIONS AND ANSWERS ABOUT CRUISES

Q. How much do cruises cost?

A. The cost is determined by a variety of factors: length of cruise, specific cruise line, type of ship, location and size of cabin, and number of people per cabin. The price can vary from $100.00 to $700.00 a day per person. There are discount rates for groups and clubs, plus off-season rates and special offers.

Q. Are cruises more expensive than other types of trips?

A. Not necessarily. It depends on which one you choose. Actually, cruises can be a good travel value if you break down all the items that are included in the cost (ports of call, meals, entertainment, services, amenities).

Q. I like sports activities. Won't I feel confined on board a ship?

A. Joggers find the open decks of a large ship good for exercise. On most ships there is an exercise room/gym, swimming pool, skeet shooting, dancing, and aerobics classes. Cruises may include several ports, with stays at destinations that have golf courses, optional diving excursions, and so on. This can break up the on board time.

Q. What about motion sickness?

A. If you are prone to motion sickness, there are many types of medication available. Your physician can advise you on the best ways to prevent and treat this possible discomfort. If you experience seasickness, stay as close to the center of the ship as possible, avoid liquids of any sort, and eat small amounts of crackers.

Q. Is an outside cabin better than an inside cabin?

A. Outside cabins have portholes and inside cabins do not, but all are temperature-controlled. Most portholes are locked. If you want fresh air, you will have to go on deck. The cabin locations subject to the least amount of sway or rolling are midship, on one of the lower decks. However, there may be more engine noise. Some ships today *only* have outside cabins.

Q. How far in advance should cruise reservations be made?

A. It is not uncommon to book a cruise six months or even a year in advance. If you want to take advantage of off-season rates, lower-priced cabins, or popular cruise dates, reserve as early as possible.

Q. I am single. Will it be a lot more expensive and will I feel uncomfortable traveling alone on a cruise?

A. Many cruise lines have special single rates, cabins, or possible share opportunities, if you are interested. The activities on board are varied and numerous; some are planned for the "unattached."

Q. I don't want to gain weight, and cruises are known for all the buffets and lavish food.

A. You can eat as little or as much as you want. Partake in on board exercises to help stabilize your weight. You may want to avoid the midnight buffets and eat lightly at meals. In addition, special diets can be accommodated if the cruise line is properly notified.

Q. We would like to take our children. Aren't cruises mostly for adults? and what about pets? Can we take our dog?

A. Several cruise lines and many ships have special activities and rates for children. An agent can check the specific details for some ships and itineraries that interest you. As far as pets are concerned, most ships do not allow them on board.

Q. What would be the best cruise ship and itinerary for me?

A. To answer that question, an agent needs to know whether you've been on cruises before, which ships you have experienced, the length of cruise you desire, what ports you would like to visit, how much you anticipate spending, what activities you enjoy, and other qualifying questions.

Q. What about tipping?

A. Cruise lines vary as to tipping guidelines and suggested amounts. If the cruise line indicates that tipping is appropriate, the amount can range from $7.50 to $10.00 per person per day, divided among the cabin steward, restaurant steward, and bus person. Additional tipping may be recommended for the maître d' and other service staff.

Q. Is there gambling on board ship?

A. Yes, most ships have a casino. If you are interested in particular casino games, check into what the ship offers. Some offer mainly slot machines, others have a more full casino, with blackjack, roulette, poker games, and so on.

Q. Can I take a cruise one way?

A. Most cruises are offered on a round-trip basis only. An agent can research possibilities of one-way or port-to-port service, depending on where you are interested in traveling.

Q. What about smoking?

A. Most ships have smoking and non-smoking areas. Many dining rooms are completely non-smoking. There is at this time one ship that is completely non-smoking, Carnival Cruise Line's *Paradise*.

Q. What about communications? I can't afford to be completely out of touch with my business.

A. Ship-to-shore communications are available and some ships now offer Internet access and other electronic services.

Q. I am afraid I will be bored, as I am not interested in sports activities or shows, games, and movies.

A. Now more than ever, cruise lines have introduced new programs that feature learning and lectures, plus health and wellness. There may be language, wine, and cooking classes. And, depending on the ports of call, there may be incredible sightseeing and cultural experiences to enjoy.

Q. Is there a "best" time to take a cruise?

A. To take advantage of lower prices there are off-season/low-season rates offered by most cruise lines. These special periods are generally when vacationers/tourists are fewer in number (such as right after or right before a holiday period). It is important to note that weather conditions are a factor—for example, hurricane season in the Caribbean is from May to November.

THE CRUISE VACATION!

At the Airport

Check in for the flight at least 90 minutes prior to domestic flights, two to three hours prior to international flights. Be sure to carry with you a picture ID and other necessary documentation (passport, visas, etc.). Upon arrival, in the baggage claim area of the airport there may be cruise line personnel to assist you with the transfer—particularly if passengers have booked an air/sea program. If not, take applicable transportation (shuttle services, taxis, etc.) to the port.

Embarkation

About two to three hours before sailing, embarkation begins. The passengers arrive, porters take baggage, and agents check tickets. Information cards must be filled out; identification and documents are reviewed. Sometimes passports are collected. Credit card information may be taken to process charges on board. The passengers may be given an identity card to use as identification and for on board charges. The maître d' may be available at this time for dining room and seating assignments (unless table reservations have already been designated).

All Aboard

Passengers are shown to their cabins by stewards. Luggage usually arrives later. Passengers are free to walk around the ship to check out facilities, or lounge on deck or in the public areas. There may be a lunch buffet available or other food service. It is helpful to have a carry-on bag with some essentials and maybe a change of clothes to start enjoying the cruise ship facilities.

Emergency Lifeboat Drill

Just after departure there will be a drill for emergency and safety procedures that passengers attend.

Actvities/Program

Passengers receive an activity program daily providing information and specifics on board the ship. The "Welcome Aboard!" sample for the S/S Sea Adventurer is one example.

Disembarkation

The last night of the cruise is when passengers are usually instructed to have their luggage placed outside their door by 3:00 A.M. for porters to pick up and take to a holding area. Breakfast on the morning of disembarkation is usually earlier and may be a limited menu. The passengers assemble in a lounge area and are told when they can disembark. Norwegian Cruise Line's "freestyle" cruising offers a more leisurely disembarkation procedure.

NOTE: The worst part of a cruise is getting on and off the ship! As you can imagine, with hundreds of people (maybe more than a thousand passengers), organizing and processing is a big procedure! Try to have reading materials and other ways to pass the time while waiting. Bring a cruise carry-on with items such as a swimsuit, change of clothes, personal items, and camera and film. And try to relax!

The daily program is usually placed in your cabin or slipped under your door every day. There are usually extra copies available at the purser's office.

S/S SEA ADVENTURER

WELCOME ABOARD!

Thank you for having chosen our ship! If there is anything we can do to make your cruise more enjoyable, please let us know!

—the Captain, Officers, and Crew

DRESS FOR THIS EVENING: CASUAL (Please no shorts or T-shirts in the dining room)

1:30 P.M.—Embarkation begins.

4:00 P.M.—All aboard for DEPARTURE!

4:00 P.M. to 5:00 P.M.—Tea/coffee and snacks are served poolside, weather permitting.

5:00 P.M. to 5:45 P.M.—Music in the Seaside Lounge for your pleasure.

5:45 P.M.—Emergency procedures drill—all passengers bring life jackets.

6:00 P.M.—FIRST SITTING DINNER in the Caribbean Room.

7:30 P.M.—Entertainment Extravaganza! Join us in the Porpoise Room.

8:00 P.M.—SECOND SITTING DINNER in the Caribbean Room.

9:30 P.M.—Entertainment Extravaganza! Join us in the Porpoise Room.

10:00 P.M.—Casino gambling available.

11:00 P.M.—Music continues in the Seaside Lounge.

11:30 P.M.—The late show "Big Star Kid" in the Cinema.

12:00 Midnight—Midnight Buffet in the Wayward Lounge.

Sunset 5:52 P.M.

TV Programming

Channel 2 Port Information

Channel 4 General Information, 24-hour Cruise Travelogues

Channel 6 Local Programming—View from the Bridge with weather and temperature

Channel 10 News Channel—CNN 24 hours

Channel 12 Movie Channel

       3:30 P.M. Cold Comfort Farm

       5:30 P.M. Toy Story II

       7:30 P.M. Grumpier Old Men

       9:30 P.M. Richard III

CHAPTER 1, REVIEW 3

Note: Some questions are repeated here for emphasis.

1. Embarkation usually begins about _____ hours prior to sailing.

2. Name four facilities available on most cruise ships. _____

   _____

3. Name three sports activities available on most ships. _____

   _____

4. The average amount required to tip the cabin steward, waiter, and bus person is $_____ to
   $_____ per person per day.

5. Name four specifics that determine the cost of a cruise. _____

   _____

6. What does "open seating" mean? _____

   _____

7. Give sample times for the late/second sitting dining:
   Breakfast_____ Lunch_____ Dinner_____

8. Most cruise lines will not accept personal checks for on board charges. True or False. _____

9. How far in advance should cruise reservations be made? _____

   _____

10. Name three items that are included in the cost of a cruise. _____

    _____

11. What are two ways/measurements that can be used to examine a ship's services? _____

    _____

12. Around-the-world cruises can take about _____ days.

13. What can you recommend to a passenger who is worried about motion sickness? _____

    _____

14. Passengers should check in at least _____ minutes prior to domestic flights and ___ to ___ hours prior to
    international flights.

15. Is an outside cabin better than an inside cabin? Why or why not? _____

    _____

CRUISE INDUSTRY TRENDS AND CHANGES

Changes continue to take place in the cruise industry. Growth, company mergers, and exciting progress in ship designs, cruise features, and itineraries are just part of the picture. A great deal of data has been compiled and there are estimates for future trends and figures, as provided by the Cruise Lines International Association (CLIA).

- The cruise industry has tripled in size every 10 years.

- The industry is young—an estimated 36 million passengers have taken cruises since 1970 and 70% of those were generated from 1980.

- Market potential is huge, with an expected 10 million passengers per year.

- Cruise products are diversified, with a type of cruise vacation available for just about everyone.

- Cruises rate extremely high as far as performance and satisfaction, when compared to other leisure travel.

- 63 new builds are on order through 2005! Newly built ships usually cost a minimum of $350 million each!

- The top cruise destination markets are the Caribbean, Alaska, the Mediterranean, Europe, trans-canal (Panama), Mexico, and Bermuda.

- Mega-ships and small boutique ships will dominate the next generation of new builds.

- Mega means mega when you're talking about a ship that's 102,000 tons with a passenger capacity of 3,315!

The newest concept in cruising, the World of ResidenSea, is expected in 2002 to offer a three-year fixed itinerary of world cruises. The 44,000-ton ship carries 285 passengers, plus a crew of 252. Residents choose from 110 "apartments" ranging from 1100 sq. ft. to 3200 sq. ft. in size. And there is a choice of six floor plans. Prices range from $2 million to $7 million and apartments are sold by invitation only. In addition to the apartments there are 88 guest suites aboard—for information, contact 1-800-970-6601 or <http://www.residensea.com>. Fares for the guest suites range from $5,000 to $35,000 per person, depending on itinerary and suite. Fares cover air fare, alcohol, tips, and port charges. Guests will also be able to buy blocks of days aboard the ship to use during a period of 24 months. Blocks of 30, 60, 100, and 200 days are available. A second ship has reportedly been ordered for delivery in 2003.

A little history: Here are some of the company mergers and changes since 1980:

1983—Cunard and Norwegian American Cruises merged to become Cunard

1984—Norwegian Cruise Line, Royal Viking Line merged to become Norwegian Cruise Line

1985—Chandris, Fantasy Cruises merged to become Celebrity/Fantasy Cruises

1986—Cunard, Sea Goddess Cruises merged to become Cunard Sea Goddess

1986—Eastern Western, Sundance Cruises merged to become Admiral Cruises

1987—Ocean, Pearl Cruises of Scandinavia merged to become Ocean Cruise Line

1987—Windstar Sail Cruises, Holland America Line merged but still operate separately

1988—Royal Caribbean purchased Admiral Cruises

1988—Princess Cruises purchased Sitmar Cruises

1988—Carnival purchased Holland America and Windstar

1993—Delta Queen Steamboat purchased American Hawaii Cruises

1995—Delta Queen Steamboat changes the name to American Classic Voyages Co.

1995—Sun Line and Epirotiki Cruises become Royal Olympic Cruise

1996—Regency Cruises ceases operations

2000—Premier Cruise Line ceases operations

2000—Cape Cananveral Cruise Line ceases operations

2001—Renaissance Cruise Line ceases operations

2001—American Classic Voyages Co. files for bankruptcy

Introducing the Queen Mary 2

In 2004, Cunard Line will introduce the Queen Mary 2, the first new ocean liner built in a generation. At a cost of $800 million, she will be the largest, longest, widest, and tallest passenger vessel ever. To get an idea of her size, the Queen Mary 2 will be as tall as a 23-story building and 1,132 feet long (nearly four football fields!). The ship will be 150,000 tons and carry 2,620 passengers. The crew numbers 1,250, assuring a luxurious service standard. A space ratio of 57.25 will allow numerous intimate venues as well as grand-scale environments. Nearly three-fourths of the cabins will have generous 8-foot balconies overlooking the sea. Cabin configurations start at 194 square feet on up to two-story duplex apartments of more than 1,650 square feet (which feature their own private gymnasiums). Combinations connecting top category accommodations can result in truly opulent quarters of 2,000 to 5,000 square feet. The Queen Mary 2 will be reminiscent of the grand ocean liners of the past, with sweeping staircases, soaring public rooms with domed ceilings, and a broad teak promenade deck all the way around the ship. She will be technologically advanced, with advanced stabilization and quiet pod propulsion. The ship will be able to cruise at 30 knots, significantly faster than other cruise ships. She will also feature intriguing items such as a planetarium, sophisticated computer systems and a multitude of activities, enrichment programs, and entertainment. Additional information can be obtained at <http://www.cunardline.com>.

CHAPTER 2

An In-Depth Look at Cruises

HIGHLIGHTS OF THIS CHAPTER INCLUDE:

- ✦ Cruise Specifics from A to Z
- ✦ Special Needs Passengers
- ✦ Documentation, Health, and Safety
- ✦ Officers and Ship Personnel
- ✦ Nautical Terms

CRUISE SPECIFICS FROM A TO Z

Aboard Ship Details—A daily activities sheet is provided to passengers. Review the information previously covered.

Air/sea Programs—Air/sea programs combine flights with cruises. However, the cruise lines sometimes book inconvenient air schedules for passengers. Also, in most cases itineraries are not given out until 30 to 45 days prior. For an extra fee (such as $35.00 a person), some lines offer an "air deviation," where a client can request a nonstop flight (if there is one) or a particular airline or airport. If the cruise company can't accommodate the request, they refund the fee. If the cruise line has to buy the ticket outside its block of seats, the price is passed on to the customer. Different names are used by the cruise lines for this service, such as "Custom Air" at Celebrity Cruises and "Seabird Gold" at Princess Cruises. Princess Cruises provides itineraries 60 days in advance. If the itinerary is not suitable to clients, they can pay the $35.00 and request the service they want (however, this may incur added charges for the tickets involved). One of the benefits of using the air/sea program is that cruise lines are aware of passengers and their flights, so if there are delays the cruise line makes every effort to accommodate the passengers (such as holding the ship if there is a large number of passengers involved or maybe even flying the passengers to the first port of call).

Alcoholic Beverages—Alcohol is only served to passengers of legal age (usually minimum age 21). Cruise lines are not liable for any actions or activities of passengers who have consumed, purchased, or obtained alcoholic beverages. Passengers may not be permitted to bring alcoholic beverages/bottles of liquor on board the ship (purchases may be collected and given to the passengers when disembarking from the cruise). Passengers may also be prohibited from consuming duty-free liquor purchased on board while on the cruise.

Babysitting—Check with the particular cruise line and ship for this service, along with children's activities. A sample cost would be $3.00 per hour for one child, and $5.00 per hour for two or more children in the same family (group babysitting service). Generally, the group babysitting service is not available for children under the age of 2.

Baggage Allowance—Most ships do not have strict limits as to the amount of baggage per passenger, but some international airlines limit the passenger to a maximum of 44 pounds (most U.S. airlines permit passengers to have two checked bags weighing up to 70 pounds each).

Baggage Liability—Most cruise lines are not liable for any loss, theft, or damage to a passenger's baggage or personal effects, unless there has been negligence on the part of the cruise line. Baggage insurance can be purchased to offer some protection. Jewelry and valuables should be left at home or entrusted to the purser's office or safety deposit boxes, if available.

Beauty Salon/Barbershop—Most ships have this service available, with applicable charges.

Bon Voyage Parties—Many ships can arrange these parties and some travel agents may order bon voyage gifts for their clients through concession companies. Confirm any arrangements in writing and usually allow at least two weeks' notice.

Cancellations and Refunds—If a passenger has to cancel, most lines will offer a full refund if the cancellation is made at least 60 days prior to sailing. Between 60 days and 30 days, they may charge a $200.00 per person fee. Between 30 and 15 days, a penalty of 50% of the fare is customary. For cancellations made between 15 days and 24 hours prior to sailing, there is usually a 75% penalty; and if the cruise is cancelled within 24 hours of sailing, normally no refund is available. Trip cancellation insurance is recommended if there is a chance of illness that might result in cancelling.

Changes—It may be possible to change the sailing date, depending on the cruise line, but a fee may be assessed for this privilege. A change of cabin assignment may be possible at no charge (depends on cruise line).

Clothing—Most cruises are informal, with casual wear suggested for day activities. Bathing suits generally should not be worn in dining rooms. There may be gala affairs on board when more formal wear (jackets for men, evening dresses for women) is suggested. At destinations it is advisable to wear comfortable shoes, as walking may be required, and to *not* wear scanty clothing or bathing suits, as local customs may tend to be conservative.

Communications—See *SHIP-TO-SHORE COMMUNICATIONS* and *TELEPHONES*.

Credit Cards—Most ships accept credit cards for purchases made in the shops on board. Some accept credit cards for payment of the cruise reservations and other on board charges.

Customs—Returning U.S. residents can bring certain amounts of duty-free purchases, depending on the destinations involved.

Duty-Free Goods

Returning U.S. residents can bring $400.00 worth of duty-free goods from an international journey ($600.00 from many Caribbean and Central American destinations*) and 1 liter of liquor (if of legal age). From a trip to U.S. Territories, residents can bring back $1,200.00 worth of goods and 4 liters of liquor. You have to have been out of the country for at least 48 hours, and the exemption may only be used once in 30 days. There are exceptions to the time limit if you travel to U.S. Territories, Mexico, and Canada. Gifts can be mailed duty-free if they are not worth over $50.00. In addition, certain items may be exempt from duty under the Generalized System of Preferences (GSP). This system helps stimulate the economy of developing countries. If you exceed the amount of duty-free goods, the tax is usually 10% up to the first $1000.00 of purchases. When traveling to other countries, find out what restrictions are made for entry to the country. Usually passengers clear customs at the first point of entry into a country.

*The beneficiary countries include Antigua and Barbuda, Aruba, Bahamas, Barbados, Belize, British Virgin Islands, Costa Rica, Dominica, Dominican Republic, El Salvador, Grenada, Guatemala, Guyana, Haiti, Honduras, Jamaica, Montserrat, Netherlands Antilles, Nicaragua, Panama, St. Kitts and Nevis, St. Lucia, St. Vincent and the Grenadines, Trinidad and Tobago.

Customs—Local customs or social practices vary. Obtain tour or guidebooks and learn what is appropriate. The cruise director usually presents information about ports and local practices.

Deck Chairs—Although a limited number may be available, there is usually no charge for their use.

Diets—Special diets can be requested. Requests should be made in writing at least four weeks prior to sailing and reconfirmed with the cruise line prior to embarkation. Certain diets may be too restrictive for the cruise line to provide.

Dining—See sample sitting times and menu and previous details.

Disembarkation—Usually takes one to two hours after docking.

Electric Current—Many ships have standard U.S. outlets. Ask the cruise line if adapters are necessary.

Embarkation—Usually begins two to three hours prior to sailing.

Entertainment—Cruise ships usually feature a variety of activities: gambling, card and game rooms, skeet shooting, a pool, a sauna, an exercise room, a theater for movies, and variety nightclub shows that follow dinner. Some have television sets, radios, and/or VCRs in the cabins. Some also have computers on board for passengers' use. New facilities can include ice-skating, rock-climbing, and more unique activities (with additional fees required).

Film Developing—Some cruises have photo developing services available and even offer a video diary for cruise passengers to purchase. These services have charges. See also PHOTOGRAPHY.

Gambling—Most ships have a casino, but check with the cruise line if you are interested in particular games, since some ships mainly feature slot machines.

Internet Service—Some ships offer Internet service/computer centers for passengers to use. Charges range from $0.75 to $1.00 per minute.

Itineraries—One of the more significant recent developments is the trend to nontraditional home-ports and ports of call. Boston has grown from a mini-cruise port to one handling over 80 cruise ship visits a year. Ports of call in the Caribbean now include places in Nicaragua, Costa Rica, Belize, and Honduras (to name a few).

Laundry Service—Except for dry cleaning, laundry service is available on most ships.

Lido Deck—The Lido Deck is often where pools and sunbathing activities are available. It's often the location of casual dining alternatives.

Lifeboat Drill—The lifeboat drill is required for passengers to have an understanding of emergency procedures. There is usually a chart on the back of the stateroom door showing the route to take from the cabin to the appropriate muster station.

Massage Services—A masseuse/masseur is usually available for this service; generally a fee is charged.

Medical Services—A qualified physician and small hospital room is provided on most ships. Any serious health problems need to be discussed with the cruise line. See the information on special needs passengers provided in this manual. Passengers are advised to carry extra prescriptions, eyeglasses, or contact lenses in case they are needed.

Option Date—The option date is the date by which payment must be made or the reservations will be cancelled.

Passengers with Special Needs—Written notification should be made to the cruise line within 14 days of reservations, and all pertinent information and specific needs should be obtained and discussed with the passenger. Refer to the information on special needs passengers provided in this manual. Cruise lines reserve the right to withhold passage from anyone who may, in the sole judgment of the cruise line, require treatment, care, or attention beyond that which the crew and ship's facilities can safely provide. See the pages in this chapter on special needs cruise passengers.

Pets—Most ships do not permit pets on board.

Photography—Most cruises have a photographer on board who takes photos of passengers in several environments. These photos are then on display and available for purchase. Photo developing may be available on the ships (usually expensive). Some cruises now feature a video diary for sale, which highlights the cruise ship's entertainment, activities, and other details.

Pregnancy—Passengers in advanced pregnancy (six months or more) must have a medical certificate from their physician.

Promenade—This is the walking area of the ship.

Religious Services—Many ships have a chapel and conduct a non-denominational service on Sundays. Wedding ceremonies are possible on some ships—check with the cruise line.

Repositioning—As certain ships change locations for seasons, they offer "repositioning" cruises. For example, some ships will relocate to the Caribbean in winter and to the Mediterranean or Alaska in summer. Rather than sail with just the crew, the cruise lines offer the one-way sailing as a special segment.

Ship Registry and Crew—The country of registry is not usually the same as the nationality of the crew.

Ship-to-Shore Communications—Generally this is available through the purser's office. Some ships have phones in the cabin that can be used. There may also be Internet access available on computers on board ships (see Internet information provided earlier).

Shore Excursions—There may be sightseeing tours and activities offered to cruise passengers. These are purchased while on board the cruise, with a form provided or through the purser's office/tour desk. Sometimes a "shore excursion package" is available prior to the cruise. A company called Port Promotions and Services of Plantation (Florida) pays travel agents 10% commission on all shore excursions purchased by their clients and 15% commission on all pre- and post-cruise packages. For more information, call (800) 929-4548 or visit their web site at <http://www.portpromotions.com>.

More About Shore Excursions

It's important to review the specifics of the shore excursions that are offered on a cruise. Sometimes passengers book a shore excursion and are disappointed in it. Other times passengers find out that they could have done the same thing on their own for much less. When reviewing the specifics of shore excursions, find out if they are a good value or if there are alternative ways of doing the activity for less. Emphasize that the cost of the excursion isn't the only consideration. The reliability and safety of the operator have to be taken into account. Maybe the excursion could be booked locally for less, but it means waiting in line, not being able to reserve the times desired, not having enough time to return to the ship before it sails, having to take transportation to/from the operator's headquarters, and so on. Pre-book shore excursions if possible to avoid on board lines, hassles, and the possibility of a "sell-out." Find out about ports of call in advance to know what sightseeing opportunities are available. Buy a good guidebook that offers information on the sights and what to expect. Find out if there are any physical requirements for the excursions. A walking tour may not seem a challenge until you find out that it's a 1,000-foot climb to the top of a cliff! Consider organizing a small group of passengers to share a taxi for a more affordable option. Realize that going on your own in some parts of the world may not be advisable. If you are going to be away from the ship during lunchtime and/or are watching your budget, ask your waiter for a box lunch to take with you (usually requires 12-hour notice). Dress comfortably and wear comfortable shoes—sandals or open shoes are not always best for exploring and sightseeing. Bring sunscreen, film, water (if applicable), and carry only essential valuables (identification, a small amount of cash/travelers' checks and maybe a credit card).

Security—You may see personnel that are part of a ship's security or they may be undercover. Report any problems to the purser's office. Stateroom doors may have peepholes for security.

Sports—Most ships have ping-pong tables, shuffleboard, skeet shooting, a pool, game rooms, and so on. New ships may have unique features such as ice skating rinks and rock-climbing walls.

Telephones—Some ship cabins may have phones. Generally, ship-to-shore communications are available through the purser's office. You may also be able to receive telephone calls on board. Telephone and fax numbers are available from the specific cruise line.

Tipping—See the general guidelines given on page 00.

Valuables—The purser's office can secure valuables and may have safety deposit boxes available.

Weddings—Weddings can be performed on some ships—check with the cruise line.

Carnival's Vacation Guarantee

Carnival Cruise Line is the only line at present that offers passengers a "vacation guarantee." It allows passengers to terminate a cruise if they are dissatisfied for any reason and receive a refund for the unused days at sea, as well as return airfare to the ship's original port of departure.

SPECIAL NEEDS PASSENGERS

Cruises offer a comfortable and enjoyable vacation opportunity for special needs travelers. Travel agents servicing clients with limitations must research the answers to some important questions.

From the Client or His or Her Aide, Determine The Following:

What is the nature of the disability?

Do you use a walker, cane, crutches, or a wheelchair?

Can you transfer yourself from a wheelchair to a seat?

What is your age, height, weight?

Will a special diet or oxygen be required?

If mentally handicapped, is the client self-sufficient?

From the Cruise Line:

If the client is in a wheelchair, how does the passenger go aboard?

Do they enter on the gangplank that may have ledges or bumps, or can they enter through the cargo hold on a smoother, wider plank?

Are the doorways wide enough to accommodate the wheelchair?

Is there room to maneuver in the bathroom?

Can the wheelchair make a turn in the bathroom? Are there handrails in the bathroom for assistance?

Are there risers or "lips" at the entrance to cabins, bathrooms, public areas, or alleyways?

Are the elevators convenient and in good working order?

Does the ship dock at ports of call, or are tenders used to carry passengers ashore?

Will disembarking at the port be uncomfortable or inconvenient? Is the dock area near enough to shops, sights, activities, and so on?

Are there any particular hazards or safety precautions that apply?

One of the most important things to do when reserving a cruise for a traveler with special needs is to provide as much information as possible. Most people with limitations are experienced at accepting and handling minor inconveniences. But there should be no major surprises.

Make certain to go over the deck plan thoroughly, and passengers should fully understand the "terms and conditions" of the cruise reservation and ticket.

The more advance planning and information exchange, the better. This will result in the more successful cruise experience that will bring repeat business and personal recommendations.

DOCUMENTATION, HEALTH, AND SAFETY

U.S. citizens taking a cruise to the Bahamas or the Caribbean need to carry proof of citizenship (preferably a passport). A voter's registration or birth certificate can be used as proof of citizenship. A driver's license is not proof of citizenship, but it will probably be necessary as photo ID, and for renting a motor scooter or a car at ports of call. U.S. Customs requires persons leaving the country with more than $10,000 in cash or monetary instruments to complete a form. It is also advisable to register cameras, jewelry, and electronic equipment so that items taken with you are not confused with purchases made abroad. Keep all receipts. Non-U.S. citizens traveling on a cruise may need passports and visas, so check with the consulate/embassy for current documentary information. The cruise line may assist you, but it is always best to confirm directly with the government of the destination in case things have changed.

U.S. citizens traveling to other countries or areas of the world may need passports, visas, immunizations, and other requirements. Again, checking with the consulate/embassy is necessary even if the cruise line provides preliminary information.

An international driving permit may be required in some countries for car rentals. These permits can be purchased through American Automobile Association (AAA) offices in the United States. On arrival at ports, a form may have to be completed and retained until passengers board the ship for departure—a type of "landing card" for disembarking and embarking. On returning to the United States, a customs form must be completed. Generally, one form is completed for a family traveling together. Review the information given previously under customs and duty-free goods. Remember not to bring any plants, fruits, vegetables, seeds, meats, or pets, as well as any banned materials, such as ivory and tortoiseshell products. Check with U.S. Customs for questions and problems.

Always look carefully at your tickets and other documentation to make sure everything is correct.

Check with your doctor regarding any health considerations and travel plans. If you are prone to motion sickness, the Transderm Scop patch, a time-released anti-motion sickness drug, can be adhered to the skin behind your ear. There are also over-the-counter medications, such as Dramamine and Bovine, as well as acupuncture "bracelets."

Use common sense about sunbathing. Use sunscreen products, a hat, and sunglasses for protection. If you are currently on any type of medication, make sure to carry it with you in the labeled bottle so there's no question as to the contents. Do not pack it in your luggage. Purchase medical insurance if you want the extra protection should an illness or emergency occur.

Cruise ships are inspected by the U.S. Public Health Service, and the Centers for Disease Control sends out inspection test summaries. The member lines of the International Council of Cruise Lines (ICCL) are required to adhere to mandatory standards on crew and passenger safety, security, environmental practices and sanitation.

The Health of Cruise Ships

The CDC (Center for Disease Control) does a twice yearly inspection of all passenger ships that sail from U.S. ports. The CDC rates cruise ships on the following items: water, food preparation and handling, potential contamination of food, and general cleanliness, food storage, and so on. For a free copy of the latest sanitation report, write the National Center for Environmental Health, Attn: Chief of the Vessel Sanitation Program, 1015 North America Way, Room 107, Miami, FL 33132, <http://www.cdc.gov>.

Participate in the lifeboat drill, follow procedures, and take appropriate safety measures. BON VOYAGE!

OFFICERS AND SHIP PERSONNEL

The officers and administrative personnel on most ships include the following:

Captain—Master of the ship. He or she directs the ship, officers, and crew and is the host of the CAPTAIN'S PARTY/DINNER (held on a specific night of the cruise).

Chief Engineer—Supervises the running of the engine room.

Chief Purser—Like a hotel manager. The purser and staff provide banking services, mail, and ship-to-shore telephone/communications (which may also be available from your cabin). Sometimes the purser's office is also where shore excursions are booked and paid for. Generally, the purser's office handles problems and questions.

Chief Steward—Supervises all cabin services.

Ship's Doctor—Provides medical services needed (applicable charges apply).

Cruise Director—Usually not an officer, the cruise director should be available and visible to the passengers. He or she acts as a master of ceremonies and may also give lectures, seminars, advice, assistance, and information.

The officers are usually uniformed and may be a different nationality than the crew.

The crew and other personnel who service passengers include: **CABIN STEWARDS, RESTAURANT STEWARDS/WAITERS, BUSBOYS, MAÎTRE D' AND ASSISTANT MAÎTRE D'S, WINE STEWARDS, BARTENDERS, ENTERTAINMENT AND ACTIVITIES STAFF, SHOP ATTENDANTS/CASHIERS, AND CASINO STAFF.**

PREFIXES TO SHIP NAMES
(Letters may follow shipname with or without a slash /)

CV—Container Vessel	SB—Steamboat
DS—Diesel Ship	STR—Steamer
MS—Motor Ship	SS—Steamship
MTS—Motor Turbine Ship	SV—Sailing Vessel
MV—Motor Vessel	TS—Turbine Ship
MY—Motor Yacht	TSS—Turbine Steam Ship
NV—Nuclear Vessel	TV—Turbine Vessel

CHAPTER 2, REVIEW 1

1. If a person has to cancel a cruise reservation, most cruise lines offer a full refund if the cancellation is made at least _____days prior to sailing.

2. Clients' valuables should be entrusted to the _____ or safety deposit boxes, if available.

3. Name four entertainment activities available on cruises. _____

_____

4. Do ships permit pets on board?_____

5. What documentation can be used as proof of citizenship? _____

_____

6. Disembarkation usually begins about _____ hours after docking.

7. Returning from Caribbean destinations such as Aruba, Jamaica, and Grenada, U.S. residents can bring back $_____ worth of duty-free goods.

8. Plants, vegetables, fruits, seeds, meats, or pets cannot be taken out or brought back into the United States. What are two banned materials that are also mentioned? _____

9. Sightseeing tours and activities that are offered at ports are called _____

_____.

10. The _____ acts as a master of ceremonies and is usually available at all times to the passengers.

11. MV stands for _____ .

12. Ship-to-shore communications can be made through the _____ as well as sometimes from the cabins.

13. MS stands for _____ .

14. SS stands for _____.

15. As certain ships change location for seasons, they offer _____ cruises.

NAUTICAL TERMS

Aft—The rear of the vessel.

Alleyway—A passageway or corridor.

Amidship—In or toward the middle of the ship.

Astern—In, at, or toward the rear of the vessel.

Backwash—Water thrown back by a ship's passage.

Bareboat charter—A charter without a crew.

Beam—The width of the ship at its widest part.

Bearing—Compass direction, expressed in degrees, from the ship to a particular destination.

Bells—Audible sound of ship's time—one bell for each progressive half-hour to a total of eight, commencing at half-past the hours of 4, 8, and 12.

Berth—Bed, usually attached to a wall; also a space where a ship docks.

Bilge—The bottom of a ship from the keel to where the sides start to rise.

Binnacle—A case containing a ship's compass, with a lamp for use at night.

Boatswain—Ship's officer in charge of sails, rigging, and the like.

Bosun—An abbreviation for boatswain.

Bow—The front part of the ship.

Bridge—The captain's work area, from where the ship is steered.

Brigantine—A two-masted vessel.

Bulkhead—Any of the partition walls that separate parts of the ship.

Bulwark—A ship's side above the upper deck.

Buoy—A warning float or marker indicating a navigable channel (pronounced "boo-eee" in the United States, but also pronounced "boy").

Capstan—Motor-driven spindle used for winding in cables.

Cleat—A device used to secure cables or ropes.

Coaming—Raised partition at the base of doorways to prevent water from entering.

Colors—A national flag or ensign flown from the mast or sternpost.

Companionway—A stairway, such as those between decks.

Containerships—Containers or boxes for carrying cargo.

Crows Nest—A platform high on the mast of a ship.

Davit—A device on a ship used for hoisting lifeboats or the anchor.

Debark—To disembark, to get off, to go ashore.

Deck Plan—The diagram of a ship showing cabins, public areas, and so on.

Disembark—To get off the ship, to go ashore.

Dock—Structure to which a ship attaches itself.

Draft—The depth of water a ship draws.

Embark—To go aboard.

Even Keel—The ship in a stable vertical position.

Fantail—The rear or aft overhang of a ship.

Fathom—A measure of length, approximately 6 feet, used chiefly in determining the depth of water.

Fore or *Forward*—Toward the bow of the vessel.

Free Port—A port free of customs duty and other customs regulations.

Freighter—A ship that mainly carries cargo, but may also carry a limited number of passengers.

Funnel—The smokestack, or chimney, of a ship.

Galley—A ship's kitchen.

Gangway—Where you leave and enter the ship.

Gross Registered Ton—A measure of the cubic content of the enclosed space on a ship (a measure of size). 100 cubic feet enclosed is a gross registered ton.

GRT—See Gross Registered Ton.

Gunwales—The upper edge of a ship's or boat's side (pronounced "gunnels").

Hatch—An opening on deck that leads to a cargo hold.

Hawsehole—A hole in the ship's bow for running cables through.

Hawser—A cable, often of steel, used to secure or tow a ship.

Head—Toilet facilities.

Helm—Apparatus by which a ship is steered.

Hold—The interior of the ship where cargo is stored.

Hovercraft—A vehicle or craft that travels while being buoyed or supported by air pressure.

Hull—The outer walls of a ship.

Hydrofoil—Ship or boat that has attached struts for lifting the hull clear of the water as it gains speed.

Jacob's Ladder—A rope ladder usually with wooden rungs.

Jones Act/Passenger Services Act—This act, passed in 1886, prohibits foreign-registered ships from carrying passengers directly between U.S. ports.

Keel—A horizontal steel plate that runs along the bottom of a ship supporting the whole frame.

Knot—A unit of speed equal to one nautical mile per hour, or about 1.15 land miles per hour.

League—3 nautical miles.

Lee or *Leeward*—The direction away from the wind.

Lido—Usually an area by a pool; generally an outdoor area.

Log—Official daily record of a ship's progress.

Manifest—List or invoice of a ship's passengers or cargo.

Moor—To secure a ship to a fixed place.

Muster Drill—The process of acquainting the passengers with the ship's regulations and safety operations prior to sailing.

Nautical Mile—Approximately 6,080 feet.

Pitch—The alternating rising and falling of a ship's bow, which may occur when underway.

Plimsoll Line—A mark showing the maximum permitted load for ships carrying cargo.

Port—Left side of a ship, sometimes called larboard.

Port of Disembarkation—The destination port of a sailing or cruise, where passengers depart.

Port of Embarkation—Where passengers board a ship, the origin point.

Port Taxes—Taxes specific to the ports on a cruise itinerary, normally paid prior to sailing.

Porthole—Window.

Posh—Comes from "port outward, starboard home"—the British usage on the sailings between England and India. The choice cabins were portside leaving England and starboard on the return.

Promenade Deck—A deck area designed for walking.

Prow—Toward the front part of a vessel.

Quay—A wharf or pier. Also a dock. Quay is pronounced "key."

Registry—A ship's certificate of registration issued by a country, which does not necessarily indicate any quality of service/safety. The country of registry doesn't have to correspond to the crew's nationality.

Repositioning—When a ship moves to a new area for cruise service.

Rudder—A movable, vertical device used for steering the ship.

Running Lights—Three lights (green on the starboard side, red on the port side, white at the top of the mast) that are required to be on when a ship is in motion between sunset and sunrise.

Scupper—An opening that enables water accumulated on deck to flow overboard.

Stabilizer—Retractable "fin" that extends from the sides of the ship to reduce sway and rolling.

Stack—A tall, vertical pipe or chimney on a ship.

Starboard—Right side of the ship.

Stateroom—Cabin.

Stem—The bow of the ship.

Stern—The aft or rear of the ship.

Stowaway—An unregistered passenger; a hiding place.

SWATH—Small Water Plane Area Twin Hull; a ship design minimizing pitching and rolling.

Tender—Small boat used to carry passengers to port when the ship cannot pull up against the dock, also may be used as a lifeboat.

Transderm Scop—A band-aid like patch placed behind the ear to prevent motion sickness discomfort.

Tug—A vessel equipped with heavy-duty engines, used for towing.

Wake—The waves or smooth water caused by the motion of a ship passing through water.

Waterline—The line on the side of the ship's hull corresponding to the surface of the water.

Weigh—To hoist or raise the anchor.

Windward—The direction toward the wind.

Yaw—To steer off course.

SOME ADVANTAGES AND DISADVANTAGES OF CRUISES:

ADVANTAGES	DISADVANTAGES
Cost is all-inclusive	Another type vacation could be less expensive
Unpack only once	Cabins may be small
Entertainment and shows	May not be for everyone
Special services	Sometimes a language barrier with the crew
Variety of activities	Space is limited for some sports
Variety of ports	Stays at ports can be short (a couple of hours)
Gourmet food in quantities	Not good if dietary needs/a weight problem
Glamour, prestige, romance	Some don't offer the seclusion people seek
Enjoy the climate and weather	If bad weather occurs, no control/alternatives
Fresh air and the "at sea" experience	Motion sickness causes discomfort
Gambling	Expensive if you gamble, drink liquor
Relaxing, an atmosphere of getting away from it all, friendly environment to make acquaintances	You may not like the people around you and the ship may be crowded
Can be a safer type of vacation	Sometimes not available on short notice, some need reservations far in advance

CHAPTER 2, TEST 1

Define the following terms:

1. Gangway _____

2. Aft _____

3. Gross Registered Ton _____

4. Hold _____

5. Freighter _____

6. Leeward _____

7. Bridge _____

8. Starboard _____

9. Knot _____

10. Port _____

11. Windward _____

12. Tender _____

13. Hovercraft _____

14. Hydrofoil _____

15. Beam _____

16. Draft _____

17. Bow _____

18. Hull _____

19. Deck Plan _____

20. Galley _____

CHAPTER 3

Freighters, Ferry Services, and Chartering a Boat

HIGHLIGHTS OF THIS CHAPTER INCLUDE:

- ✦ Freighters
- ✦ Ferry Services
- ✦ Chartering a Boat

FREIGHTERS

Freighter travel is quite different from cruise travel. Freighters carry cargo, which is their most important item. Ports and itineraries are subject to change. Even the point of departure can change, even up to a few days before sailing. There are some luxury cruise-freighter ships, but generally freighters can be characterized as follows:

- Voyages generally longer in duration than those of cruises

- Carry only about 12 to 15 passengers

- Normally do not have formal entertainment, but may have lounges, a library, a pool, a sauna, and laundry facilities

- May change itinerary, ports, and length of trip; may experience delays

- Require passengers to be in good health, since most do not have a doctor on board (some require a physician's letter)

- May have age limits (maximum age 75 on some, up to age 82 on others)

- Can be inexpensive for the number of days involved

- May have long waiting lists (some reservations are booked more than a year in advance)

- Might be available for one-way transportation

- Offer a unique type of sailing experience—quiet, informal, peaceful, and different ports of call

Companies to Contact for Booking Freighter Travel:

Freighter World Cruises, 183 South Lake Ave. #335, Pasadena, CA 91101, (800) 531-7774 or (626) 449-3106, <http://www.freighterworld.com> handles reservations for more than 23 international shipping lines that operate more than 100 ships. Some of the lines/ships they represent include: Bank Line, Columbus Line, Chilean Line, Martime Reederei, Rickmers Reederei, Reederei Bernhard Shulte, Schepers, Grimaldi Freighter Cruises, H. Buss and Oltmann, NSB, TIM Shipping Line, Mineral Shipping, Egon Oldendorff, Leonhardt and Blumberg, Niederelbe Schiffahrtsgesellschaft Buxtehude, Projex Line, and Transeste Schiffahrt Gmbh.

Maris Freighter Cruises, 215 Main St., Westport, CT 06880, (800) 99-MARIS, (203) 222-1500, Fax (203) 222-9191, <http://www.freightercruises.com>.

Travltips, Cruise and Freighter Travel Association, P.O. Box 580188, Flushing, NY 11358, (800) 872-8584, e-mail: <http://info@travltips.com>, <http://www.travltips.com>.

The Cruise People, LTD. Located in London, this company represents 350 ships.

Freighter Travel LTD—located in New Zealand.

A search on the Internet for freighter travel will also provide companies/agents/contact information.

A sample itinerary and specifics for a freighter trip are shown at the top of the following page.

Sample Freighter Trip Information

Schulter line (German ownership, Cyprus registry) offers service from Long Beach, California, with anticipated calls to Pusan, South Korea; Kaohsiung, Taiwan; Hong Kong; Pusan (2nd call), South Korea; Manzanillo, Mexico; Panama Canal transit; Manzanillo, Panama; Savannah, Georgia; Norfolk, Virginia; New York; Felixstowe, England; Bremerhaven, Germany; Rotterdam, Netherlands; Le Havre, France; New York (2nd call); Norfolk, VA (2nd call); Savannah, Georgia (2nd call); Manzanillo, Panama (2nd call); Panama Canal transit; Manzanillo, Mexico (2nd call); returning to Long Beach. U.S. coast-to-coast segment not available without European or Asian call. Segments are available. Approximate duration: 90 days. Maximum passengers: 7. Fare range (per person): About $6,300 to $8,415. Age limit: 79.

The commission to travel agents on freighters varies from 7% to 10%.

On a freighter you can enjoy quiet days at sea in informal and casual surroundings. No crowds, no formalities—just comfort, relaxation, sun, clean air, casual dress, a small number of passengers who love the freedom from clocks, and the chance to do what they want when they want. The only scheduled activities are mealtimes. Most ships have spacious, well-furnished outside cabins with private baths. There is usually a self-service bar for a daily cocktail hour, maybe a small pool, and good deck space. Freighter travel is a great value, with fares typically ranging from $65.00 to $125.00 a day. The majority of freighter cruises are from 30 to 75 days, but some are two to three weeks.

Here is a brief list of FREIGHTER LINES AND THEIR DESTINATIONS:

Bank Line	*South Africa, Europe, Southeast Asia*
Chilean Line	*U.S. East Coast, Africa's west coast*
Columbus Line	*World*
DSR	*World*
Ivaran Lines	*U.S .East Coast and Gulf Coast to South America*
Leonhardt and Blumberg	*United States, Far East, and Suez Canal*
Martime Reederei	*U.S. West Coast to the Mediterranean*
Mineral Shipping	*Singapore, Croatia, Bahamas, U.S. East Coast, Netherlands*
Projex Line	*Mediterranean, Panama Canal*
Schepers Line	*Caribbean*
Schulter Line	*Asia, Far East*
Transete Shipping	*Caribbean*

Books about Freighter Travel

One of the best references for comprehensive freighter information is *Ford's Freighter Guide.* Other resources include *The Freighter Travel Manual* by Bradford Angier and *Freighter Voyaging* by Robert B. Kane and Barbara W. Kane. These may be available through bookstores or the Internet. Some freighter companies and information can also be found in the *Official Cruise Guide.*

Vessel Types

Mail and Supply Ships: Typical of this type of vessel is the *RMS St. Helena* that sails from the United Kingdom to South Africa, and the Ascension, Canary, and St. Helena islands. These ships carry mail, cargo, and supplies to out-of-the-way destinations.

General Cargo Ships: Prior to containerization, all cargo was carried on general cargo ships. The cargo was known as break-bulk cargo. With container ships now sailing, there are fewer general cargo ships. These ships are used when the cargo is too large to fit in containers (such as steel, rolls of wire, and machinery) or boxed goods are too small to justify the use of a full container. General cargo ships take longer to load and unload and thus have longer port times. A variation of the general cargo ship is a banana boat—a ship whose only purpose is to carry bananas.

Containerships: Also known as "box" ships, these ships carry containers that are generally 20 to 40 feet long. They can be filled with any type of cargo. The containers that carry frozen or chilled food are known as "refers," or refrigerated containers. Containerships' capacities are measured in technical equivalent units (TEUs). For example, a freighter with a capacity of 1,600 TEUs is small when compared with one of the largest containerships in the world, the *Regina M,* which carries about 6,600 TEUs.

Expedition Ships: These ships carry between 52 and 177 passengers on voyages to the Antarctic, South Georgia and the Falklands, Patagonia, islands of the South Atlantic, the Amazon, Iceland, Greenland, the Northwest Passage, Hudson Bay, plus the Lost Islands of the South Pacific, Polynesia, Melanesia, and the Russian Far East.

Bulk Carriers: These ships carry coal, grain, phosphates, and other "loose" cargo.

Coasters: Small cargo ships are called coasters. They run on feeder routes and carry a small number of containers from small ports to major ports. They are called coasters because they travel along the coast, making many stops in a short period of time.

Ro-Ros: These ships carry motor vehicles, which are loaded via a stern ramp. They can be quickly loaded and unloaded with a large number of vehicles. Ro-Ro stands for roll on, roll off.

Tankers: Passengers do NOT travel on tankers, not only because of the risk, but the smell of oil is quite overwhelming.

Words of Wisdom About Freighter Travel

Don't be tempted to buy a special fare/excursion ticket for travel to your embarkation point. The schedules of freighters are constantly subject to change. The booking agents make every attempt to keep passengers advised of schedule changes, but never assume that no news means nothing has changed. Stay in touch with the agent and make that last call to see if there have been any last-minute adjustments.

Once in the port city, passengers should call the line's agent to confirm their arrival, and learn about the location and embarkation details. If the contact agent is a local agent in the port city, this individual is a cargo agent with no responsibility for the passengers. Questions pertaining to the ship, itinerary, or any other trip details should be directed to the booking agent or the personnel aboard ship.

Expect the unexpected and ride the changes to the itinerary or other ship specifics.

Did You Know?

• Author Alex Haley wrote much of the book *Roots* at sea on a freighter.

• Most container ships do not have elevators.

• The water you drink and bathe with is made on board the vessel.

• The maximum width of a ship passing through the Panama Canal is 32.2 meters. Such vessels are referred to as "Panmax."

• No passengers are allowed to travel on oil tankers.

• All items purchased aboard ship (while on the high seas) are tax-free.

• Depending on where the vessel obtains supplies, a case of Coke will be more expensive than a case of beer.

• A "scupper" is a small hole in the deck or walkway that allows rain and sea water to drain off.

• A ship can be arrested. If the vessel has incurred a liability, such as unpaid crew wages, damage to a maritime structure, or a personal injury or death, plus a number of other possible reasons, legal action is brought against the vessel. A U.S. marshall can arrest the vessel.

 SAMPLE VOYAGES

To give you an idea of the length of various voyages:

15 days and under—Transatlantic voyages generally fall in this category. Canada Maritime from Montreal to northern Europe—8 to 12 days. Schepers Line from Miami to the Caribbean—10 to 12 days. Bergen Line along the coast of Norway—12 days.

15–30 days—Special expeditions offers exploration and adventure cruising from 1 to 4 weeks. From England to South Africa—15 to 20 days. St. Helena Shipping Line from Cardiff, Wales, to Cape Town, South Africa—22–35 days. Ivaran Line from the U.S. Gulf to Central America and the Caribbean—about 21 days.

30–45 days—Rederei Nord from the U.S. West Coast to South America—30 days. NSB from U.S. West Coast to Korea and Taiwan—34 days. Grimaldi Freighter Cruises from England to Europe and South America—about 42 days. Bank Line from South Africa to India—45 to 50 days. Chilean Line from New Orleans and Houston to the West Coast of South America—about 45 days. Columbus Line from the U.S. West Coast to Australia and New Zealand—about 49 days. NSB from Antwerp, Belgium, to the Indian Ocean and East Africa—about 56 days.

60 –90 days—NSB from the U.S. West Coast to the Mideast—62 days. NSB from Europe to the Far East—63 days. Mineral Shipping from Savannah, Georgia, to the Mediterranean—60 days. From Europe to Australia and New Zealand—84 days. P & O Nedloy around the world from England—82 days.

FERRY SERVICES

There are many ferry services available between countries and for port-to-port travel. Maps will sometimes show ferry services, costs, and whether automobiles can be transported. Twice a year, Worldwide Ferry Services (P.O. Box 40819, Providence, RI 02940, (508) 252-9896) publishes a comprehensive listing. Also, the *Official Cruise Guide* provides information on some ferry services. *Thomas Cook's European Timetable* contains some European ferry service schedules, but it is mainly a reference for rail schedules. Thomas Cook also prints a *Guide to Greek Island Hopping*, providing information on ferry services to all the islands, including links to other eastern Mediterranean areas. Thomas Cook guides are sometimes available in bookstores, or you can contact Thomas Cook Publishing at P.O. Box 227, Peterborough, UK PE3 8BQ (01733) 505821/268943. Forsyth Travel Library, 9154 W. 57th St., Box 2975, Shawnee Mission, KS 66201, (913) 384-3440/(800) 367-7984, also distributes many of these guides.

The tourist information offices for the states, islands, or countries involved can usually offer assistance in ferry service information. Some ferry services are seasonal, and advance reservations as well as prepayment may be required.

There are HOVERCRAFT services between Dover, England, and Calais, France, and this service across the English Channel only takes about 35 minutes.

Some ferry companies and their services are as follows:

ADRIATICA DI NAVIGAZIONE Italy-Albania/Greece/Croatia

AG EMS Germany/Netherlands-Friesian Islands

AGAPITOS EXPRESS FERRIES Greek Coastal

ALASKA MARINE HIGHWAY SYSTEM Alaskan Coastal

ANEK LINES Italy-Greece, Mainland Greece-Crete

AUTO BATAM FERRIES Singapore Coastal

BC FERRIES British Columbian Coastal

BORNHOLMSTRAFIKKEN Bornholm-Danish Mainland

BRITTANY FERRIES United Kingdom-France/Spain, Eire-France

BUQUEBUS Argentina-Uruguay

CALEDONIAN MACBRAYNE U.K. Coastal (Hebridean and Western Isles to mainland)

CAPE MAY–LEWES FERRY Delaware, U.S. Coastal (across bay)

CAREMAR Italian Coastal

CEBU FERRIES CORPORATION Philippines Coastal

THE COHO FERRY United States-British Columbia

COLOR LINE Norway-United Kingdom/Denmark/Germany

CORSICA, SARDINIA, AND ELBA FERRIES France/Italy to Corsica, Sardinia, and Elba

CROSS SOUND FERRIES New England Coastal

DANE SEA LINE Greek Islands

DFO Germany-Sweden

DSB (a railway company that also operates Danish Coastal Services and Denmark-Sweden/Germany)

ESTLINE Estonia-Sweden

FAABRG-GELTING LINIEN Denmark-Germany

FERRIMAROC Spain-North Africa

FIRE ISLAND FERRIES Long Island to Fire Island

LINEAS FRED OLSEN Inter-Canary Islands Services

GA FERRIES Greek Islands, Southern Italy-Greece

GOTLANDSLINJEN Gotland-Swedish Mainland

GRIMALDI GROUP Italy

HELLENIC MEDITERRANEAN LINES Italy-Greece

HOVERSPEED United Kingdom-France

HURTIGRUTEN Norwegian Coastal

IRISH FERRIES Eire-United Kingdom/France

ISLAND FERRIES TEO Arran Islands-Mainland Eire

ISLE OF MAN STEAM PACKET Isle of Man-United Kingdom/Eire

ISLES OF SCILLY STEAMSHIP COMPANY English Coastal (Isles of Scilly-Mainland)

JADROLINJA Croatia-Italy/Greece, Croatian Coastal

JOHN O'GROATS FERRIES Orkney Islands-Mainland Scotland

KANGAROO ISLAND SEALINK Australian Coastal (Kangaroo Island-Mainland)

LAKE CHAMPLAIN TRANSPORTATION CO. New York-Vermont

LAKE MICHIGAN CAR FERRY Michigan-Wisconsin

MARINE ATLANTIC Eastern Canadian Coastal, Labrador-Newfoundland, Canada-United States

MERSEY FERRIES English Coastal (River Mersey Crossings)

MINOAN LINES Italy-Greece, Greek Coastal

MOBY LINE Italy-Corsica/Sardinia

MOLS LINEN Danish Coastal

NORDO-LINK Denmark-Sweden

NORTH CAROLINA FERRIES North Carolina Coastal

NORTHUMBERLAND FERRIES Eastern Canada Coastal-Nova Scotia-Prince Edward Island

P & O EUROPEAN FERRIES United Kingdom-France/Spain/Northern Ireland

P & O SCOTTISH FERRIES Scottish Coastal, United Kingdom-Norway

POLFERRIES Poland-Denmark/Sweden/Finland

PRINCE OF FUNDY CRUISES Nova Scotia-Maine

RED FUNNEL England Coastal (Isle of Wight-Mainland)

SAREMAR Italian Coastal

SCANDINAVIAN SEAWAYS UK–Netherlands/Germany/Denmark/Sweden, Denmark-Norway-Sweden

SCANDI LINE Norwegian Coastal

SCANDLINES Denmark-Sweden

SEACAT SWEDEN Denmark-Sweden

SEAFRANCE United Kingdom-France

SEAWIND Sweden-Finland

SILJA LINE Finland-Sweden/Germany/Estonia

SIREMAR Italian Coastal

SMYRIL LINE Faroe Islands-Denmark/Norway/Iceland/United Kingdom

SNCM FERRYTERRANEE France-North Africa/Corsica/Sardinia, Italy-Corsica

SPIRIT OF TASMANIA New South Wales-Tasmania

STENA LINE United Kingdom-Eire/France/Northern Ireland/Netherlands, Denmark-Sweden/Norway, Sweden-Germany/Poland

STRINTZIS Italy-Greece, Greek Islands

SWANSEA CORK FERRIES United Kingdom-Eire

SWEFERRY Denmark-Sweden/Germany, Danish Coastal

SYDNEY HARBOUR FERRIES Sydney Harbour Crossings

TALLINK Estonia-Finland

TARBERT FERRIES Irish Coastal

TIRRENIA NAVIGAZIONE Italy-Tunisia, Italian Coastal

TOREMAR Italian Coastal

TRASMEDITERRANEA Spain-Morocco, Spanish Coastal

TRUCKLINE United Kingdom-France/Spain, Eire-France

TT LINE Germany-Sweden

VICTORIA LINE United States (Washington State)-Canada (British Columbia)

Spotlight On the Alaska Ferry System

Contact the Alaska Marine Highway System, Homer Ferry Terminal, P.O. Box166, Homer, AK 99603. (907) 235-8449 or (800) 382-9229. Fax: (907) 235-6907. Services the ports of Haines, Homer, Wrangell, Ketchikan, Juneau, Sitka, Petersburg, Skagway, Cold Bay, Kodiak, Dutch Harbor, King Cove, Seldovia, Chignik, Sand Point, Seward, Whittier, and other points.

Frequently Asked Questions about the Alaska Ferry System

What are the most popular trips? From Bellingham, Washington, or Prince Rupert, British Columbia, northbound to Haines, Alaska, or Skagway, Alaska. From Valdez, Alaska, across Prince William Sound to Whittier and into Portage on the AK Railroad. From Homer, Alaska to Dutch Harbor, Alaska.

How far in advance should reservations be made? As early as possible. Some sailings are full two months or more in advance.

Can I get off the ferry? Passengers have a limited amount of time at each port—average time is one to two hours.

Is there a senior rate? Persons age 65 or older travel between specific ports for half-price on four specific vessels—*Aurora, LeConte, Bartlett,* and *Tustumena.* There is no senior rate for travel between Valdez and Whittier or Seward or for travel from Homer to Dutch Harbor.

What are the costs? There are three separate charges: cabins, vehicles, and passengers. Add all three together for total costs.

Where do I sleep if I don't have a cabin? In the recliner lounge area or solarium. Self-standing tents can be put on the deck of the larger vessels. Public showers and lockers are available. No sleeping is allowed on the car deck.

CHARTERING A BOAT

Cruise ships can be chartered by large companies, organizations, or wealthy individuals. Many companies also offer yachts and other boats for charter. Because the popularity of charters has increased and it's a specialized type of reservation/sale, there are "brokers," like travel agents, available to arrange a suitable boat for the party involved. If you are chartering a boat for the first time, check with magazines and shop around before making a commitment.

Be sure to obtain the specific details on exactly what will be provided, plus any recommendations, insurance protection available, and so on. Note that a "bareboat charter" is one without supplies or a crew. A "crewed" charter is one that includes the captain and crew.

Some companies are listed below with phone numbers, Web sites, and areas for charters. The list is not all-inclusive or an endorsement of any company's operations. Changes may have occurred after this book was published. You may want to consult the tourist office of the island or country for further information.

Abaco Bahamas Charters—(800) 626-5690, <http://www.abacocharters.com>, Bahamas.

Abercrombie & Kent Int'l—Oak Brook, IL, (800) 323-7308, <http://www.abercrombiekent.com>.

Bitter End Yacht Club—Chicago, IL, (800) 872-2392, Virgin Islands.

Cortez Yacht Charters—Lemon Grove, CA, (619) 469-4255, <http://www.cortezcharters.com>, southern California and Cabo San Lucas, Mexico and Zihuantanejo, Mexico.

Euro Charters—Travel by Jennie, Cocoa, Fl, (800) 950-5610, <http://www.pbyg@mindspring.com>.

EuroCruises—New York, (800) 688-EURO, <http://www.eurocruises.com>, Baltic and Scandinavia.

Florida Yacht Charters—Miami Beach, FL, (800) 537-0050, <http://www.floridayacht.com>, Miami, Bahamas, and Key West.

Nicholson Yacht Charters—Cambridge, MA, (800) 662-6066, <http://www.yachtvacations.com>.

Pacific Destination Center—Huntington Beach, CA, (800) 227-5317, <http://www.pacific-destinations.com>.

Regency Yacht Vacations—Charlotte Amalie, St. Thomas, (800) 524-7676, <http://www.regencyvacations.com>.

Russell Yacht Charters—New York, (800) 635-8895, <http://www.cruisingin paradise.com>, Worldwide charters.

SailAway Yacht Charters—Miami, FL, (800) 724-5292, <http://www.1800sailaway.com>.

St. Petersburg Yacht Charters and Sales, Inc. St. Petersburg, FL (727) 823-2555.

SUNSAIL—Ft. Lauderdale, FL, (800) 327-2276, <http://www.sunsail.com>, charters for the Bahamas, Virgin Islands, St. Maarten, Mediterranean, and Thailand.

The Charter Locker—Kailua-Kona, HI, (808) 326-2553, <http://www.aerialsportfish-ingkona.com>, Hawaii.

The Greek Island Connection—New York, (800) 241-2417.

Treasure Harbor Charter Yachts—Islamorada, FL, (800) 352-2628, <http://www.trea-sureharbor.com>, Florida Keys, Dry Tortugas, Bahamas.

Valef Yachts—Ambler, PA, (800) 223-3845, <http://www.valefyachts.com>, specializes in Greece.

VIP Yacht Charters—Largo, FL, (800) 225-2520, <http://www.vipyachts.com>, United States/British Virgin Islands.

Zeus Yacht Cruises—New York, (800) 447-5667, <http://www.zeustours.com>.

A search on the Internet produced a list of 27 boat charters Web Sites. The Web site <http://www.excite.com/travel/cruises_and_vacations/boat_charters/> listed

Aladdin Cruises	NACO
AquaSafaris	Nautica Magazine
Australian Charter Guide	New Zealand Charters
BoatNet	Port Yacht Charter
Caribbean Charters	Richleigh Yachts
Cat Sailing in the Caribbean	Sailboats, Inc.
Charterlink	Sailing and Diving Vacations
Charternet.com	Sailing Paradise
Cristal Charters	Sailing Vacations—Barrington-Hall Corp.
Cumberland Charter Yachts	A to Sea Yachting
Cyberyachts	W.G. Charters
L'Iliade	Yacht Charters
Luxury Charters of New Zealand	Yacht Charters International
Moorings	

CHAPTER 3, REVIEW 1

1. Name five ways that freighters are different from cruise ships.

   _____

   _____

   _____

   _____

   _____

2. List two references for ferry services information.

   _____

   _____

3. Container ships are also known as _____ .

4. What's a "scupper"? _____

   _____

5. Name three freighter lines and their destinations:

   _____

   _____

   _____

6. What's a bareboat charter? _____

   _____

7. Name a popular trip on the Alaska Ferry System. _____

   _____

8. Give three destinations of expedition ships. _____

   _____

9. Containerships are measured in TEUs. What does TEU stand for? _____

   _____

10. Why do tankers not take passengers? _____

    _____

CHAPTER 4

Cruising Areas and Ports

HIGHLIGHTS OF THIS CHAPTER INCLUDE:

- ◆ Cruising Areas of the World and Ports of Call
- ◆ Ports of the United States and Canada
- ◆ Bermuda
- ◆ Ports of The Caribbean
- ◆ Ports of Mexico
- ◆ Ports of South America
- ◆ Some Ports of Europe
- ◆ Scandinavia
- ◆ The Greek Islands
- ◆ Ports of Africa
- ◆ Ports of Asia
- ◆ Ports of the Pacific

CRUISING AREAS OF THE WORLD AND PORTS OF CALL

Bahamas—Popular for three- and four-night cruises from Port Canaveral, Miami, and Ft. Lauderdale, and included on some seven-day cruises.

Bermuda—Seven-day cruises from New York and Philadelphia are usually operated from late April to early October, sometimes repositioning the ships to the ports of Miami or Ft. Lauderdale for the rest of the season.

Western Caribbean—Visiting ports in the Bahamas, possibly Jamaica, the Cayman Islands, and the Yucatan peninsula of Mexico.

Eastern Caribbean—Possibly stopping at the British Virgin Islands, Puerto Rico, the U.S. Virgin Islands, St. Kitts, St. Maarten, Dominica, and so on.

Southern Caribbean—These visit ports such as Aruba, Bonaire, and Curacao, plus Barbados, Martinique, and St. Lucia.

Mexico—Popular ports include Acapulco, Puerto Vallarta, Cozumel, Cancun, Cabo San Lucas, and Mazatlan.

Alaska—Cruises through the inside passage offer sightseeing of Glacier Bay National Park, Haines, Skagway, Juneau, Sitka, Wrangell, Misty Fjords National Monument, Ketchikan, and so on. They may begin or end in Anchorage or Vancouver, British Columbia, Canada.

Hawaii—Seven-night cruises round-trip from Honolulu or a stop on a Pacific cruise. Ports of call include Honolulu on Oahu, Kahului on Maui, Kona and Hilo on the big island of Hawaii, and Nawiliwili on Kauai.

United States and Canada, Eastern Seaboard—New England and Canada's Maritimes offer beautiful scenery, tiny fishing villages, and the historic St. Lawrence Seaway, with ports such as Boston, Halifax and Sydney in Nova Scotia, and ports in the province of Quebec.

United States and Canada, West Coast—Major U.S. ports are Los Angeles, San Diego, and San Francisco. Depart Seattle and Vancouver, British Columbia, Canada, for Alaska cruises.

United States and Canada, Inland Waterways—Cruise the Mississippi River in a steamboat, or explore the Columbia and Snake rivers in the U.S. Pacific Northwest, or cruise the St. Lawrence Seaway and Hudson River in the Eastern Seaboard. Inland waterway cruises are often used to reposition the ships from their winter schedule in the Caribbean to their summer schedule in the Northeast.

The Panama Canal—Transit takes one day, with the rest of the cruise usually stopping in Acapulco and other Mexican ports.

South America—Some itineraries combine Caribbean ports of call with navigation of the Amazon River. Caracas, Venezuela, and Cartagena, Colombia, are often-visited ports.

Scandinavia and Northern Europe—This area offers the popular ports of Amsterdam (Holland); Bergen, Oslo, and Tromso (Norway); St. Petersburg (Russia); Copenhagen (Denmark); and Helsinki (Finland).

Western Mediterranean—Ports include Ajaccio or Bonifacio on Corsica (France); Barcelona (Spain); Capri, Venice, Naples, Florence, Taormina, Portofino, Genoa, and Civitavecchia (Italy); Palma on Mallorca or Ibiza in the Balearic Islands (Spain); Monte Carlo (Monaco); Malta and Lisbon (Portugal); plus stops at Casablanca (Morocco), Funchal on Madeira (Portugal), the Canary Islands (Spain), and more.

Eastern Mediterranean—Lots of stops in the Greek Islands, plus the opportunity to visit numerous ports of Turkey (Istanbul, Kusadasi, Bodrum, Canakkale, and Dikili—to name a few). Black Sea cruises may stop at Odessa and Yalta (Ukraine).

Africa—Pass by 6,000 years of civilization sailing on the Nile River in Egypt. Choose from small yacht-like vessels accommodating about 20 passengers to larger, more luxurious vessels that hold about 80 passengers. Other stops in Africa are probably in conjunction with an around-the-world cruise.

Indian Ocean—Featuring the Seychelles Islands, with stops perhaps on Madagascar, or ports of India (Bombay, Goa, Madras, Cochin), or Sri Lanka.

The Orient—Cruises of the Orient can depart from Singapore, Hong Kong, or Beijing (China).

Southeast Asia—Bangkok (Thailand), Jakarta (Indonesia), and Penang (Malaysia) are frequent stops.

Oceania, South Pacific Islands—Ports in French Polynesia that are the most popular are Papeete (Tahiti), Moorea, Huahine, and Bora Bora.

When Is the Best Time to Go?

For the Caribbean, Mexico, Hawaii, the Orient, and some other areas—cruises are available all year. Here is a short list of areas and seasons for cruising:

Africa—Year-round, but mostly May–October for North Africa, November–April for Eastern and Southern Africa

Alaska—May–September

Asia and the Orient—October–March

Baltic, Bermuda, the Black Sea, and Canada—May–October

Caribbean, Hawaii—Year-round

India and Southeast Asia—Year-round, but mostly November–April

Mediterranean—March–November

Mexico—Year-round

New England—May–October

Panama Canal—September–May

South America—Northern Coast—year-round; other areas—September–April

South Pacific—Year-round but mainly November–April

PORTS OF THE UNITED STATES AND CANADA

Miami (Dodge Island), Florida

Ft. Lauderdale (Port Everglades), Florida

Port Canaveral, Florida

Tampa, Florida

St. Petersburg, Florida

Palm Beach, Florida

Norfolk, Virginia

Baltimore, Maryland

New York, New York

Boston, Massachusetts

Los Angeles, California

Cincinnati, Ohio

Memphis, Tennessee

Nashville, Tennessee

New Orleans, Louisiana

Philadelphia, Pennsylvania

Pittsburgh, Pennsylvania

St. Paul, Minnesota

San Francisco, California

Seattle, Washington

Chattanooga, Tennessee

Charleston, South Carolina

Warren, Rhode Island

St. Louis, Missouri

Portland, Oregon

San Diego, California

Wilmington, North Carolina

Redwood City, California

Washington, D.C.

Honolulu, Hawaii

Anchorage, AK (other Alaskan ports include Whittier, Seward, Sitka, Dutch Harbor, and Juneau)

Vancouver, BC, CANADA (other Canadian ports include Quebec City, Halifax, and Montreal)

General Information

This list does not include the many cities from which there are ferry services.

Mississippi and Ohio River cruises on the Delta Queen or Mississippi Queen steamboats are popular. There are three-, four-, five-, and seven-day itineraries available, with departures from cities such as Chattanooga, St. Paul, Cincinnati, Memphis, Nashville, New Orleans, St. Louis, and Pittsburgh.

Many Caribbean cruises and cruises to the Bahamas leave from the ports of Miami and Ft. Lauderdale. Port Canaveral, Tampa, and Palm Beach are additional cruise departure points. Cruises in the Northeastern United States are less crowded and less expensive than Alaska cruises, and offer beautiful scenery, historical sights, tiny fishing villages, and some wildlife (including whales). Some ships only offer a couple of cruises between their summer season in Europe and their winter season in the Caribbean.

Cruises through the inside passage of Alaska are very popular. A detailed map of this area is provided on page 53 after the exercise to identify ports of the United States and Canada. From May to October, cruise ships carry visitors through the 1,000-mile long inside passage of coastal British Columbia and southeast Alaska. There are round-trip cruises and combination cruise tours.

The Alaska Marine Highway ferry liners operate port-to-port services, carrying vehicles as well as passengers between many points.

USING THE LIST AND AN ATLAS IF NECESSARY, IDENTIFY THE PORTS (1–32):

1. _____

2. _____

3. _____

4. _____

5. _____

6. _____

7. _____

8. _____

9. _____

10. _____

11. _____

12. _____

13. _____

14. _____

15. _____

16. _____

17. _____

18. _____

19. _____
20. _____
21. _____
22. _____
23. _____
24. _____
25. _____

26. _____
27. _____
28. _____
29. _____
30. _____
31. _____
32. _____

Details of Ports of Embarkation in North America

ANCHORAGE—The airport is about 7 miles from downtown. Passengers are generally transported by bus or train to the port areas.

BALTIMORE—This is a huge port for a relatively small city. It takes at least 30 minutes by taxi from the airport. There is parking available at the pier.

BOSTON—The port is located about 20 minutes from Logan Airport or about 10 minutes from downtown by taxi. Parking is available nearby.

LOS ANGELES—There is no parking at the pier, although areas can be found within a mile or two. It's about 30 minutes from the airport or downtown.

MIAMI—About 25 minutes from Miami International Airport, Dodge Island or the cruise port of Miami has some of the best port facilities in the world. Parking is available at the pier.

MONTREAL—Forty minutes from the airport, this port on the St. Lawrence River is within walking distance of the city's center.

NEW ORLEANS—The pier areas are about 45 minutes from the airport and parking is available nearby.

NEW YORK CITY—An hour from JFK Airport, the entrance to the New York Consolidated Passenger Ship Terminal is at West 55th Street and 12th Avenue. There is parking available at the pier.

PORT CANAVERAL—About one hour from Orlando's International Airport and 90 minutes from Disney World, Port Canaveral offers parking at the pier.

PORT EVERGLADES (Ft. Lauderdale)—Only 2 miles from the airport, this port is convenient and offers parking.

SAN DIEGO—About 5 miles from the airport, the port of San Diego is close to many attractions.

SAN FRANCISCO—About 35 minutes from the airport, the port of San Francisco offers convenient parking.

SEATTLE—About 20 miles (35 minutes) from the airport, this port is conveniently located near the city attractions and has parking available.

TAMPA—About 20 minutes from Tampa International Airport or 35 minutes from St. Petersburg/Clearwater Airport, this port city has new channelside shops and restaurants and an entertainment complex and offers parking across the street.

VANCOUVER—The airport is 45 minutes away and the port is right in the middle of this very attractive city.

Alaska's Inside Passage

From May to October, cruise ships carry visitors through the 1,000-mile long inside passage of coastal British Columbia and southeast Alaska. There are round-trip cruises and combination cruise tours.

The Alaska Marine Highway ferry liners operate port-to-port services, carrying vehicles as well as passengers between many points.

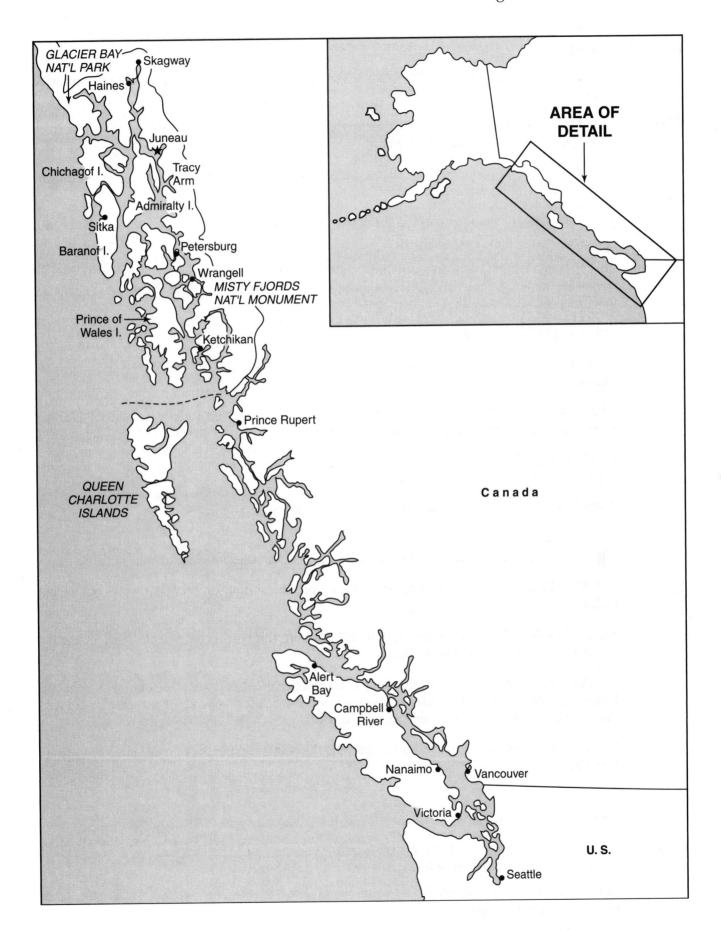

GLACIER BAY NAT'L PARK
Skagway
Haines
Juneau
Chichagof I.
Tracy Arm
Admiralty I.
Sitka
Baranof I.
Petersburg
Wrangell
MISTY FJORDS NAT'L MONUMENT
Prince of Wales I.
Ketchikan
Prince Rupert
QUEEN CHARLOTTE ISLANDS
Canada
Alert Bay
Campbell River
Nanaimo
Vancouver
Victoria
Seattle
U. S.

AREA OF DETAIL

BERMUDA

Cruises to Bermuda usually depart from New York or Philadelphia. They visit St. George's and Hamilton.

PORTS OF THE CARIBBEAN

Island group/name: major islands, cities or ports (pronunciation)

Anguilla ("an-gwil-a")
Antigua ("an-tee-ga"): St. John's
Aruba: Oranjestad
Bahamas: Nassau (on New Providence Is.), Freeport (on Grand Bahama Is.), Out Islands
Barbados: Bridgetown
Barbuda
Bonaire: Kralendijk ("kralenjik")
British Virgin Islands: Virgin Gorda, Tortola, Norman Is., Peter Is.
Cayman Islands: Grand Cayman
Curacao ("Kur-ah-sow"): Willemstad
Dominica: Roseau, Cabrits
Grenada ("gren-aid-a"): St. George's
Guadeloupe: Pointe-a-Pitre ("pwan-tah-peetra")
Jamaica: Ocho Rios, Montego Bay
Martinique: Fort de France
Montserrat: Plymouth
Netherlands Antilles—see Aruba, Curacao, St. Maarten, etc.
Nevis ("nee-vis")
Puerto Rico: San Juan
Saba ("saa-ba")
St. Barts
St. Croix ("saint croy"): Christiansted
St. Eustatius (commonly called "Statia")
St. John
St. Kitts
St. Lucia ("saint loo-sha")
St. Maarten: Philipsburg
St. Thomas: Charlotte Amalie ("charlotte am-a-lee")
St. Vincent and the Grenadines: Bequia, Kingstown, Mayreau, Tobago Cays, Union Island
Trinidad and Tobago: Port of Spain, Scarborough
U.S. Virgin Islands (see St. Thomas, St. Croix, and St. John)

Some longer cruises stop at La Guaira, the port for Caracas, Venezuela. Other stops on certain Caribbean cruises are Devil's Island (off the coast of French Guiana), the San Blas Islands of Panama, and Isla Margarita (off the coast of Venezuela). There are cruises that depart from ports such as San Juan, St. Thomas, Barbados, and Aruba.

PORTS OF THE CARIBBEAN

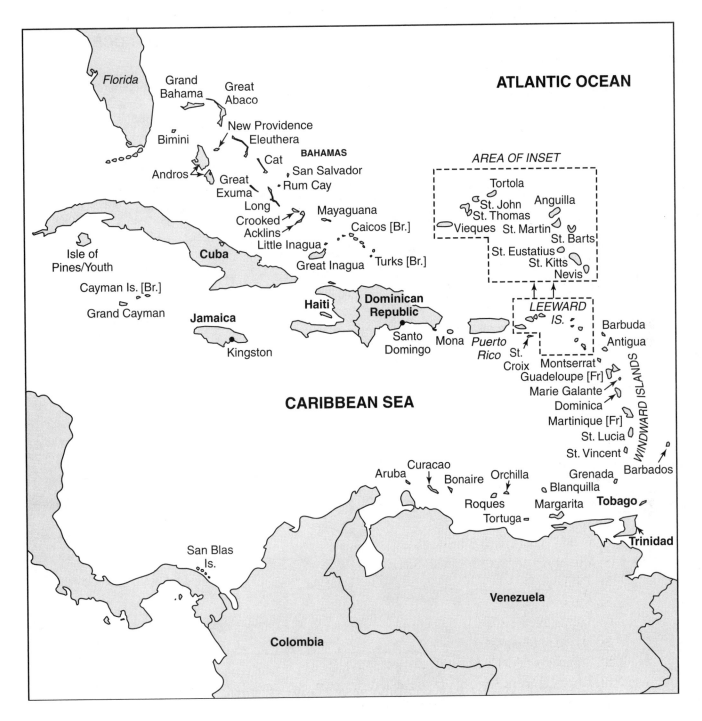

Western Caribbean Cruises

Cruises to the western Caribbean often include a stop at Key West, Florida, plus ports such as Montego Bay or Ocho Rios, Jamaica, Grand Cayman in the Cayman Islands, Playa del Carmen, and Cozumel, Mexico.

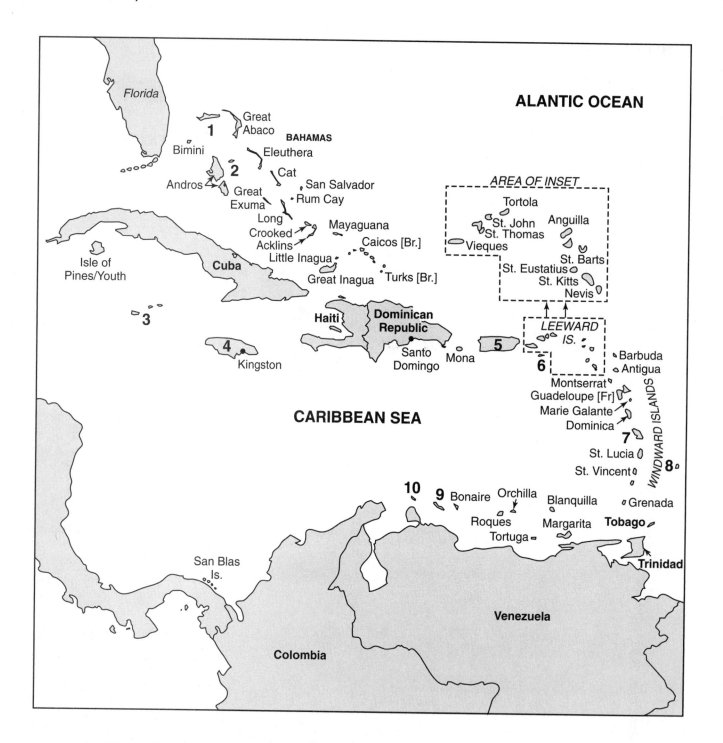

USING THE PREVIOUS MAP FOR REFERENCE, IDENTIFY THE ISLANDS THAT ARE MARKED 1–10.

1. _____   6. _____

2. _____   7. _____

3. _____   8. _____

4. _____   9. _____

5. _____   10. _____

Trans Panama Canal

Many transcanal cruises visit the San Blas Islands before the Panama Canal transit. Cristobal is the port of Panama on the Caribbean side, while Balboa is on the Pacific side. The transit takes about eight hours, during which time three sets of giant locks will raise and lower the ship 85 feet. The unique experience is accented by the verdant jungle scenery, colorful birds, and exotic wildlife.

Shore Excursions on Caribbean Cruises

Since Caribbean cruises are so popular, here are a few ports in the Caribbean with sights and activities for shore excursions.

THE BAHAMAS

Nassau, New Providence Island

Capital of the Bahamas, Nassau offers sightseeing and shopping. Points of interest include Bay Street, Straw Market, Cable Beach, nearby Paradise Island (for the beach and casinos there), the Nassau casinos, Fort Charlotte, Governor's Mansion, and the Queen's Staircase. Possible tours/activities offered by cruises include city tour, sailboat/barge trip, nightclub/casino tour, and scuba diving trip.

Freeport, Grand Bahama Island

Sights in Freeport include the International Bazaar, which features shops from around the world, Lucaya National Park (for its limestone caves and caverns), the Port Lucaya shopping and entertainment plaza, Rand Memorial Nature Center, the Grand Bahama Museum, and the Garden of the Groves (12 acres of gardens with exotic flowers, birds, and waterfalls).

PUERTO RICO

San Juan, Puerto Rico

Over 1 million passengers pass through this port annually. At present about 28 vessels use San Juan as their homeport. Puerto Rico's sights and attractions include Old San Juan (El Morro—a dramatic military fortification—is there), Fort San Cristobal, San Juan Cathedral, the Pablo Casals Museum, La Fortaleza (built in 1540 and used as an executive mansion and the official home and office of the governor of Puerto Rico), the City Wall and San Juan Gate, San Jose Plaza, the Tapia Theater, and Fort Geronimo (located outside the walls of the old city). The Bacardi Rum plant, situated across San Juan Bay and accessible by ferry, offers guided tours of its distillery, bottling plant, and museum. The University of Puerto Rico has a botanical garden featuring over 200 species of tropical and subtropical vegetation.

El Yunque Rain Forest

Located 35 miles east of San Juan, El Yunque consists of 28,000 acres of rain forest in the Luquillo Mountains, and has over 240 varieties of trees and flowers.

Ponce, Puerto Rico

Ponce, the second largest city in Puerto Rico, has over 500 restored historic buildings.

Culebra, Mona, And Vieques

These are three offshore islands noted for beautiful sandy beaches, coral reefs, and fresh seafood. Mona has some cliffs 200 feet high and Vieques has a phosphorescent bay.

U.S. VIRGIN ISLANDS

St. Thomas

The port of Charlotte Amalie on St. Thomas can be bustling with cruise passengers since many ships stop here. There are many shops, along with warehouses offering duty-free liquors, cigarettes, gold and other jewelry, perfumes, and more. Bluebeard's Castle overlooks the harbor and is a good place to stop for a banana daiquiri. Drake's Seat overlooks Magen's Bay, and numerous resorts dot the island. Coral World is an aquarium attraction that is world-famous. Swimming and diving beaches include Magen's Bay, Coki Beach, Morningstar, Limetree Beach, Sapphire Beach, and Secret Harbor.

St. Croix

The port of Christiansted is small and can only accommodate ships with less than 200 passengers. The port of Frederiksted can handle larger ships. Besides duty-free shopping, there is the Christiansted National Historic Site, which includes Fort Christianvaern, the Old Scale House, Danish Customs House, and the West Indies and Guinea Warehouse (which was once the site of the largest slave auctions in the Caribbean). Buck Island, located 2 miles off the coast, offers an underwater National Monument, plus white sandy beach and picnic areas.

St. John

St. John is the least developed of the U.S. Virgin Islands. It has no airport, and much of the island has been set aside as a national park. Cruz Bay is a small town offering gift shops and diving centers.

BRITISH VIRGIN ISLANDS

The British Virgin Islands are an archipelago of about 40 islands, but only 15 are inhabited. Tortola is the largest and is linked by a bridge to Beef Island. Road Town on Tortola is the capital of the British Virgin Islands, and has a colorful market and West Indian-style houses. The famous Baths—a unique rock formation of dimly lit caves—are on Virgin Gorda.

JAMAICA

Ocho Rios

Shopping bargains and natural wonders like Dunn's River Falls are the attractions of this port. Tours take passengers to the falls to relax or make the adventurous climb. Sightsee through Fern Gulley and visit plantations in the area, such as Prospect or Brimmer Hall.

Montego Bay

Attractions of Montego Bay include the Rose Hall Great House and Plantation, the Greenwood Great House, rafting on the Martha Brae River, the Rocklands Feeding Station (a bird sanctuary), Sam Sharpe Square for shopping, and Ft. Montego.

CAYMAN ISLANDS

Grand Cayman

Famous Seven Mile Beach and the Turtle Farm are two of the main sights on this small island full of delights. The diving here is world-famous, with wrecks, reefs, and walls. There is also the Atlantis submarine experience, Pirate Caves in Bodden Town, the Blow Holes site (to see water spraying up like geysers), and Sting Ray City (excursion by boat to hand-feed sting rays). And don't forget to go to Hell—the village where postcards mailed are postmarked from Hell!

ARUBA, BONAIRE, AND CURACAO

Aruba

Oranjestad, the capital, has museums, shops, and casinos. Visit the Natural Bridge, an arch carved from coral cliffs by the sea. There are many nice beaches, but the surf can be very rough. Old gold mining towns of Bushiribana and Balashi are other stops, as is the 540-foot peak, Hooiberg (Mount Haystack).

Bonaire

The pastel-colored buildings common to all three of these islands are sights in Kralendijk, the capital of Bonaire. A place of rest and privacy, the island is known for interesting flora and fauna, particularly birds.

Curacao

Sights in Willemstad, the capital, include the Queen Emma Pontoon Bridge (a unique passenger bridge that swings open and closed across the harbor), Fort Nassau, Fort Amsterdam (with Fort Church), the Floating Market, restored Dutch colonial buildings, and duty-free shopping. There is also the Seaquarium, Christoffel Park, Amstel Brewery, and Curacao Liqueur Distillery. There are 17th- and 18th-century plantation houses, several dive and snorkeling sites, and an underwater cave at Boca Tabla.

MARTINIQUE

Fort-de-France is the capital, and the island features attractions such as La Savane (park and gardens), La Pagarie (museum), historic churches and buildings, Mont Pelee (extinct volcano), and duty-free shopping.

ST. LUCIA

Castries, the capital, is one of the most beautifully situated cities in the Caribbean. Surrounded by hills, it has a large, safe, land-locked harbor, and it is a major port of call for cruise ships, which dock at Pointe Seraphine. Soufriere is the second largest settlement on the island. This deep-water port is situated at the foot of the Pitons, two extinct volcanoes (probably St. Lucia's most popular attraction). This island of contrast offers unspoiled beaches, rain forests, rugged mountain trails, and a visit to hot springs in one of the world's only "drive-in" volcanoes. There is considerable French influence.

BARBADOS

There are dramatic differences between the east and west coasts of the island of Barbados. The east side is less developed and rugged. The west coast (Caribbean side) has the capital, Bridgetown, and more hotel development. In Bridgetown there's a miniature copy of London's Trafalgar Square, plus Fairchild Market, St. Michael's Cathedral, the Government House, Barbados Museum, and the Old Synagogue and Cemetery. A spectacular excursion is to Harrison's Cave, an eerie, luminous cavern. There is also Ashford Bird Park, Gun Hill, St. Nicholas Abbey, Sam Lord's Castle, and the Barbados Wildlife Reserve.

ANTIGUA

Nelson's Dockyard in English Harbour is one of the safest landlocked harbors in the world. St. John's Cathedral is on many postcards and included in most visitors' photographs. Indian Town is a national park of Antigua, and the carved Devil's Bridge is to be seen there. The Heritage Quay Tourist Complex is a shopping and entertainment complex.

GUADELOUPE

On a map, Guadeloupe looks like a giant butterfly. The Riviere Salee flows between its two wings—Basse-Terre and Grand-Terre. A drawbridge over the channel connects the two islands. Pointe-a-Pitre, the port city, is a kaleidoscope of boutiques, sidewalk cafés, markets, buildings, and parks.

ST. MAARTEN/ST. MARTIN

The Dutch side is St. Maarten, the French side is St. Martin. The Dutch capital is Philipsburg, and it is situated on a sand bar that separates the Great Salt Pond from the ocean. Beach activities and shopping satisfy most tourists.

ST. KITTS

If you have four hours, you can drive around all of St. Kitts and stop at the 1694 Brimstone Hill Fortress at Sandy Point for a view of the nearby island of St. Eustatius.

NEVIS

Surrounded by coral reefs, Nevis is a 35-square-mile island with three high peaks at its center.

ST. VINCENT AND THE GRENADINES

This string of islands between St. Vincent and Grenada are among the most beautiful and least developed islands of the Caribbean. Snorkeling and water sports are wonderful here.

TRINIDAD AND TOBAGO

The capital and main port, Port of Spain, is on Trinidad. Walk through the sights and sounds of the city beginning at Queen's Wharf and north to Independence Square, Frederick Street, Queen Street, and the Red House (seat of the government). Visit the Angostura Bitters factory and the 200-acre Queen's Park Savannah area. Tobago is completely unspoiled and offers exotic bird life and a colorful market in the main town of Scarborough.

MEXICO

Playa Del Carmen and Cancun

Shopping and beach tours or a day trip to the Mayan ruins at Tulum are popular excursions. Xcarat is a beautiful eco-archeological theme park that offers a tropical exploration of the Caribbean jungle. Here you can enjoy a swim through the mysterious underground river.

Cozumel

Scuba divers and snorkelers will enjoy the beautiful reefs and waters that surround this island. There are shops and restaurants in the city of San Miguel.

Costa Maya

Located south of Cozumel on the mainland, this is a self-contained area of shops with a relaxing pool and beach area.

Cabo San Lucas

At the tip of the Baja peninsula are San Jose del Cabo and Cabo San Lucas. Sea lions frolic under Los Arcos, a natural rock arcade that is best viewed from small boats.

Acapulco

This true resort city is filled with high-rise hotels, crowded beaches, and loads of shops. Take the trip to La Quebrada to watch the cliff divers.

Puerto Vallarta

On Mexico's Pacific coast, Puerto Vallarta has shops and boutiques. Popular shore excursions include boat trips to Yelapa (a tropical fishing village with a lovely beach). Mismaloya, 7 miles south, was the site of the film *Night of the Iguana*.

Mazatlan

Also on the Pacific coast, this port features excursions to quaint villages and mining towns, plus the San Blas jungle area.

HONDURAS

Roatan

Besides an island discovery tour, excursions here include trips to Tabyana Beach, Dolphin Encounters, snorkeling and dive trips.

BELIZE

Belize City

From Belize City there are trips to Altun Ha—Mayan ruins and a cruise on the Olde Belize River. Other excursions will take you to Lamanai and the New River, to Xunantunich (Mayan ruins), or on a cave tubing adventure.

KEY WEST, FLORIDA

The southernmost city in the continental United States is nicknamed the "Conch Republic." From a walking tour of historic homes to shopping, sailing, snorkeling, diving, and fishing trips, this is a comfortable port of call. Attractions include the Key West Custom House, Mel Fisher's Maritime Museum, Hemingway Museum, Old Mallory Square, Harry S. Truman's Little White House, and, of course, loads of shops, bars, and restaurants.

Note: Because so many islands routinely feature duty-free goods, check on prices of items before leaving home, so that you can judge if the item you are buying is truly a bargain. Also, guard valuables and use common sense if sightseeing on your own. Be aware of local laws. Any approaches made by panhandlers or those peddling drugs should be ignored. Dress conservatively. Do not insult or ridicule local peoples or customs.

The Panama Canal

The approximately eight-hour transit of the Panama Canal is truly an unforgettable experience for passengers sailing between Atlantic and Pacific ports of call. Tropical scenery accompanies you on this passage through one of the largest man-made bodies of water in the world, 166-square mile Gatun Lake. Entering from the Atlantic is Limon Bay at Cristobal breakwater, just before the Gatun locks and lake. Then passengers sail through the Gaillard Cut, an 8-mile channel through solid rock. At the south end are the Miguel and Miraflores locks and the Canal Zone city of Balboa.

CHAPTER 4, REVIEW 1

1. The El Yunque Rain Forest is found on the island of _____.

2. Sightseeing from Ocho Rios, Jamaica, may include visiting _____ Falls.

3. The Queen Emma Pontoon Bridge is a sight of _____, Curacao.

4. The capital of St. Lucia is _____.

5. _____ is the port of St. Croix that can only handle small ships, while _____ can handle larger ships.

6. Noted for beautiful sandy beaches and coral reefs the three offshore islands of Puerto Rico are _____, _____, and _____.

7. If your cruise stops at Montego Bay, Jamaica, you may visit the_____ Great House or the _____Great House.

8. The Seaquarium and Christoffel Park are sights on the island of _____.

9. You would be on the island of _____ if you visited the Pirate Caves in Bodden Town and Sting Ray City.

10. The International Bazaar and Lucaya National Park can be found in/near the city of _____ _____on _____ Island.

11. Two miles off the coast of St. Croix is _____, offering an underwater National Monument.

12. Nelson's Dockyard in English Harbour is on _____.

13. A miniature copy of London's Trafalgar Square is on the island of _____.

14. The popular beaches on _____ include Sapphire Beach, Magen's Bay, Coki Beach, and Morningstar.

15. The old gold mining towns of Bushiribana and Balashi are sights on _____.

16. The Pitons, two extinct volcanoes, are probably the most popular attraction of _____.

17. The second largest city in Puerto Rico is _____.

18. _____ is the least developed of the U.S. Virgin Islands.

19. The British Virgin Islands are an archipelago of about _____ islands, _____ of which are inhabited.

20. _____, an island of rest and privacy, is known for its interesting flora and fauna, particularly birds. Kralendijk is the capital.

21. Mont Pelee is an extinct volcano found on _____.

22. You would be on _____ if you visited the city of Hell.

23. The Amstel Brewery is an attraction on Aruba. True or False _____.

24. Bay Street, Straw Market, Cable Beach, Paradise Island—these are all sights when visiting _____ on New Providence Island.

25. When your cruise stops at the port of _____, on _____ you can tour the Pablo Casals Museum and El Morro.

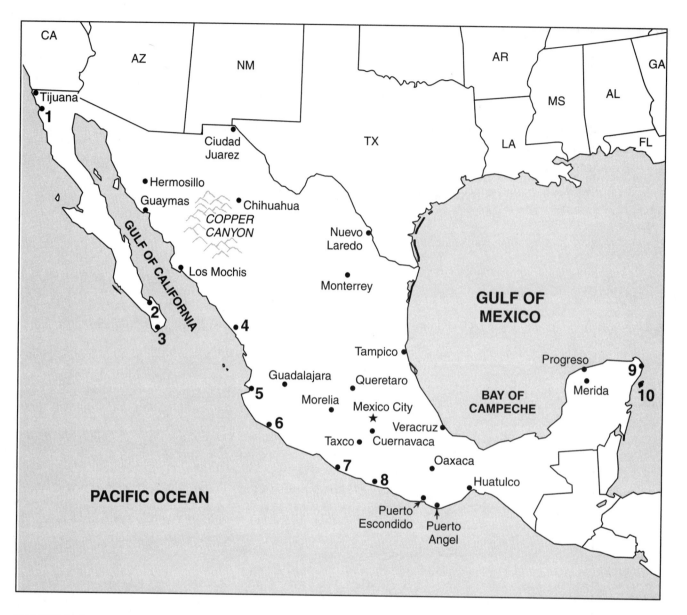

PORTS OF MEXICO

Ensenada	Veracruz	Puerto Vallarta
Zihuatanejo/Ixtapa	Tampico	La Paz
Mazatlan	Playa del Carmen, Cancun	Progreso
Cabo San Lucas	Cozumel	Guaymas
Manzanillo	Acapulco	

Note: There are a couple of excursion vessels that explore the Gulf of California, stopping at small islands and ports such as Guaymas.

The port of Acapulco offers the chance to see the world-famous cliff divers, Cozumel offers fantastic snorkeling, and Cabo San Lucas has the scenic gateway rock formations and whale watching (December–March). Some ships now stop at Costa Maya, a port south of Playa del Carmen.

USING THE LIST, AND AN ATLAS IF NECESSARY, IDENTIFY THE PORTS (1-10). Write answers on separate paper.

PORTS OF SOUTH AMERICA

La Guaira, near Caracas, Venezuela
Cartagena, Colombia
Valparaiso, Chile
Punta Arenas, Chile
Montevideo, Uruguay
Punta del Este, Uruguay
Antofagasta, Chile

Belem, Brazil
Rio de Janeiro, Brazil
Natal, Brazil
Recife, Brazil
Callao, Peru
Iquitos, Peru
Port Stanley, Falkland Is.

Buenos Aires, Argentina
Santos, Brazil
Salvador (Bahia), Brazil
Fortaleza, Brazil
Lima, Peru
Guayaquil, Ecuador
Devil's Is., French Guiana

USING THE LIST, AND AN ATLAS IF NECESSARY, IDENTIFY THE PORTS (1–14). Write answers on separate paper.

Note: South America's cruising season is short (generally from the end of December to early March). Amazon cruises include stops at Manaus and Belem in Brazil, or Iquitos and Leticia in Peru. Expeditions to the Galapagos Islands (off the coast of Ecuador) provide a chance to see unusual wildlife (tortoises, iguanas, cormorants, blue-footed boobies, sea lions, and albatross). A few expedition vessels visit the Falkland Islands (off the coast of Argentina). The approach to Rio de Janeiro by ship is one of cruising's more breathtaking sights, as you approach Sugar Loaf Mountain. There are some cruises to Antarctica, for those interested in a unique exploration and cruise experience.

PORTS OF EUROPE

Stockholm, Sweden	Copenhagen, Denmark	Naples, Italy
Helsinki, Finland	Dover, England	Genoa, Italy
St. Petersburg, Russia	Calais, France	Gibraltar
Gothenburg, Sweden	Palermo, Italy	Valletta, Malta
Bremerhaven, Germany	Ostend, Belgium	Bari, Italy
Amsterdam, Netherlands	Barcelona, Spain	Nice, France
Rotterdam, Netherlands	Lisbon, Portugal	Palma, Mallorca
Antwerp, Belgium	Venice, Italy	Hamburg, Germany
Cherbourg, France	Marseilles, France	Corfu, Greece
Southampton, England	Piraeus, Greece	Kusadasi, Turkey
Istanbul, Turkey	Malaga, Spain	Monte Carlo, Monaco

General Information

There are hundreds of ports in Europe for ferry services that carry passengers and sometimes cars.

Popular English Channel crossings are Dover to Calais, Boulogne, Ostend, and Zeebrugge. The "Chunnel," an underwater train tunnel, connects England to France.

Barge cruises are available in England, France, Holland, and Belgium. These vessels usually carry four to 50 passengers on short itineraries (generally not exceeding 50 miles) along the narrow inland waterways of their countries and occasionally out onto wider rivers.

Rhine River cruises operate from cities such as Amsterdam, Basel, Cologne, Rotterdam, and Strasbourg.

There are Baltic and Black Sea cruises, cruises around the British Isles, Danube River cruises, Moselle and Rhone River cruises, Volga River cruises, and Mediterranean and Scandinavian cruises.

Greek Island cruises are popular, and it is important to know that the port of Athens is Piraeus.

Most eastbound transatlantic cruises leave from New York and arrive in Southampton or Cherbourg.

Local spellings of many cities may differ. For example, here are a few cities and their possible spellings:

Venice = Venezia	Ostend = Oostend	Gothenburg = Goteburg
Lisbon = Lisboa	Antwerp = Antwerpen	Naples = Napoli

An exercise to identify ports of Europe is followed by detailed maps of Scandinavia and the Greek Islands.

USING THE LIST, AND AN ATLAS IF NECESSARY, IDENTIFY THE PORTS (1–30).

Note: Dotted lines indicate areas that are detailed on maps that follow.

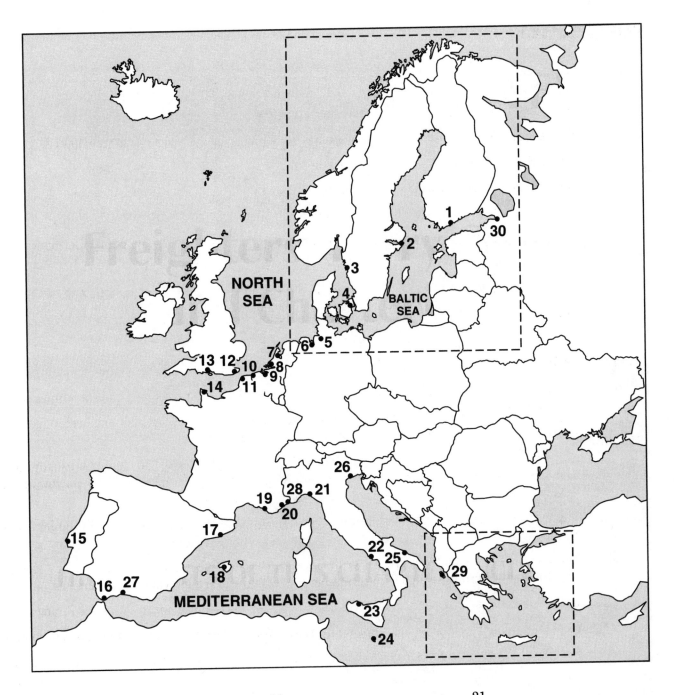

1. _____
2. _____
3. _____
4. _____
5. _____
6. _____
7. _____
8. _____
9. _____
10. _____

11. _____
12. _____
13. _____
14. _____
15. _____
16. _____
17. _____
18. _____
19. _____
20. _____

21. _____
22. _____
23. _____
24. _____
25. _____
26. _____
27. _____
28. _____
29. _____
30. _____

SCANDINAVIA

The scenery of Scandinavia is absolutely spectacular, and when combined with visits to fascinating cities such as Oslo, Stockholm, Bergen, Copenhagen, and Helsinki, it provides a memorable experience. Although the cruise season is very short (June, July, August), the itineraries feature fjords and fairy tales, the North Cape and the Midnight Sun, Scandinavia and Russia. Cruise tour vacations are popular, since they offer the chance to spend nights before or after the cruise in some of the exciting cities of Europe.

THE GREEK ISLANDS

From Piraeus, the port of Athens, ferry services are available to take passengers and sometimes vehicles to Corfu, Mikonos, Siros, Naxos, Rhodes, Samos, and other islands.

Some cruises leave Athens to ports of call such as the island of Corfu, Sicily (off Italy), Malta (below Sicily), Rhodes, Alexandria (for Cairo, Egypt), Heraklion (on Crete), Santorini, Mikonos, and Istanbul (in Turkey). The wonder of the ancient times mixes with such beautiful sights as the windmills of Mikonos and the dazzling whitewashed stone buildings of Santorini.

CHAPTER 4, REVIEW 2

INDICATE THE LETTER OF THE CORRECT ANSWER IN THE SPACE PROVIDED.

1. A popular English Channel crossing is from Dover to
   A. Dublin
   B. Paris
   C. Southampton
   D. Calais

   ANSWER_____

2. The port of Athens is
   A. Heraklion
   B. Rhodes
   C. Crete
   D. Piraeus

   ANSWER_____

3. Most eastbound transatlantic cruises leave from
   A. Miami
   B. Boston
   C. New York
   D. Norfolk

   ANSWER_____

4. Barge cruises are generally available in
   A. Germany, France, Holland
   B. France, England, Belgium
   C. Belgium, France, Germany
   D. England, France, Italy

   ANSWER_____

MATCH THE PORTS TO THEIR COUNTRIES:

Note: Some answers may be used more than once and some may not be used.

5. _____ Valletta   A. France

6. _____ Hamburg   B. Germany

7. _____ Rotterdam   C. Belgium

8. _____ Cherbourg   D. Malta

9. _____ Bari   E. Italy

10. _____ Nice   F. Holland/Netherlands

USING THE SCANDINAVIA AND GREEK ISLANDS MAPS, ANSWER THE FOLLOWING:

11. The Kiel Canal connects the North Sea to the Atlantic Ocean. True or False _____

12. The port shown for the country of Poland is _____.

13. The Gulf of _____ is between Sweden and Finland.

14. Stavanger is a major port of Sweden. True or False _____

15. Tromso is the most northern port shown in Norway. True or False _____

16. The island of Rhodes is in the group called the _____.

17. Mikonos is in the Aegean Sea. True or False _____

18. Santorini is part of a group of islands called the _____.

19. Corfu is one of the _____ Islands.

20. The port of Crete is _____.

PORTS OF AFRICA

Cape Town, South Africa
Durban, South Africa
Mombasa, Kenya
Port Said, Egypt
Conakry, Guinea

Tunis, Tunisia
Freetown, Sierra Leone
Abidjan, Cote d'Ivoire
Lagos, Nigeria
Monrovia, Liberia

Dakar, Senegal
Casablanca, Morocco
Dar es Salaam, Tanzania
Canary Islands (Spain)

Port Said is the gateway to the Suez Canal (the transit takes about 18 hours). Nile cruises are available from cities such as Aswan, Cairo, and Luxor—for four-, six-, 10-, 11-, and 14-day itineraries. The best months for cruising the Nile are September and April/May, when the days are sunny and warm and the nights are cool.

USING THE LIST, AND AN ATLAS IF NECESSARY, IDENTIFY THE PORTS (1–14). Write answers on separate paper.

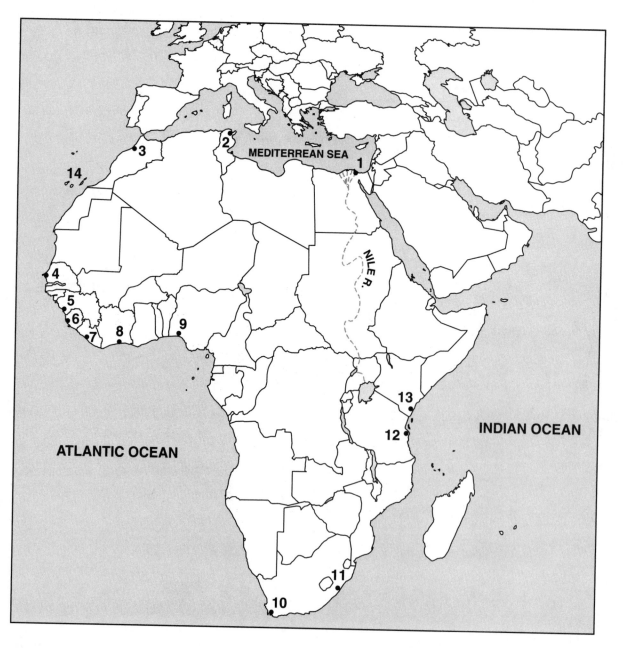

PORTS OF ASIA

Macau
Bombay, India
Madras, India

Nagasaki, Japan
Singapore
Bangkok, Thailand

Kobe, Japan
Tokyo, Japan
Shanghai, China

Manila, Philippines
Hong Kong
Pusan, Korea (South)

Cruises to China often feature cruise and tour combinations.

USING THE LIST, AND AN ATLAS IF NECESSARY, IDENTIFY THE PORTS (1–12). Write answers on separate paper.

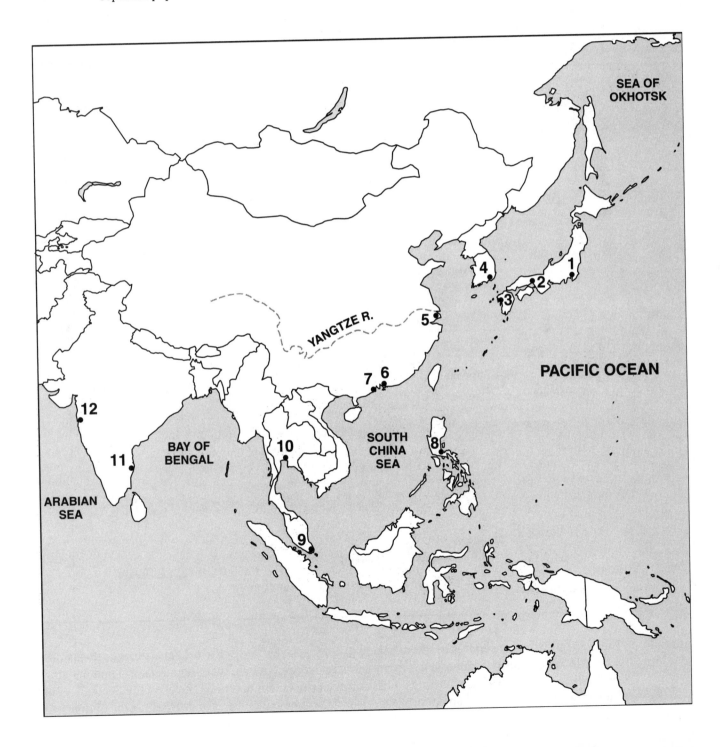

PORTS OF THE PACIFIC

Honolulu, Hawaii
Papeete, Tahiti*
Moorea, Tahiti*
Bora Bora, Society Is.*
Christmas Is., Kiribati
Pago Pago, American Samoa

Apia, Western Samoa
Suva, Fiji Islands
Nuku'alofa, Tonga
Sydney, Australia
Cairns, Australia
Darwin, Australia

Brisbane, Australia
Hobart, Australia
Wellington, New Zealand
Auckland, New Zealand
Christchurch, New Zealand
Easter Island

*French Polynesia

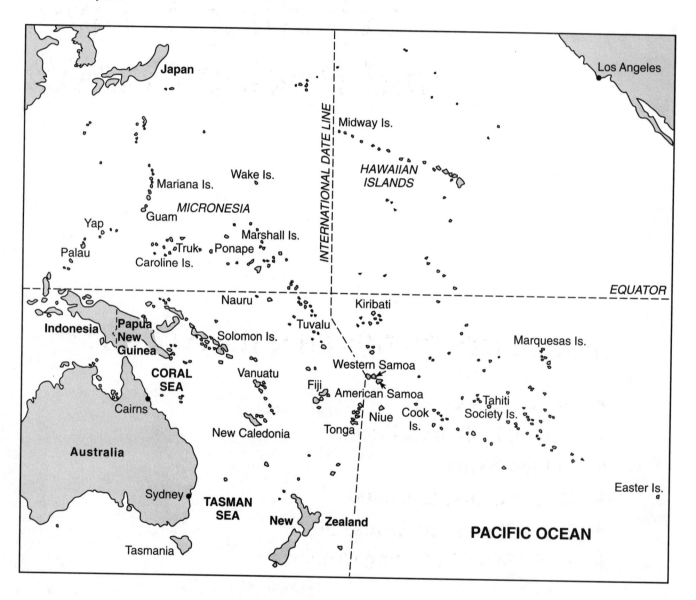

There are port-to-port services in several island groups, such as Tonga, Kiribati, and the Society Islands (which includes Tahiti). Indonesia has many services between points. Bali, Indonesia, is a popular stop on Pacific cruises, as well as a starting point for some cruises. Some cruises travel on the Sepik River of Papua New Guinea, offering an opportunity to visit the unusual cultures and tribes people of this area of the world.

CHAPTER 5

Selecting, Selling, and Pricing Cruises

HIGHLIGHTS OF THIS CHAPTER INCLUDE:

- ✦ Selecting a Cruise
- ✦ Selling to Today's Clients
- ✦ Selling Skills
- ✦ Which Cruise to Choose
- ✦ Cruise Lines and Cruise Ships
- ✦ Basic Steps in Selling Cruises

SELECTING A CRUISE

Selecting the right cruise for a client involves many factors:

- Whether a specific cruise ship or cruise line is desired
- Length of cruise
- Cruise departure point; cruise area or destinations
- Client's budget
- Dates of travel preferred, any alternatives
- Destinations the client is interested in visiting
- Whether the client has been on a cruise before; if yes, what ships
- Client's likes, dislikes, expectations of services
- Any special needs or requirements*

If clients don't have a particular ship or cruise in mind, start with a question such as, "What length of cruise interests you?" The primary factors (*budget, length,* and *dates*) will focus on an initial selection, and the other items of information are necessary for further recommendations or decisions. For example, if a couple wants a seven-day Caribbean cruise, the agent can begin by stating that prices begin at about $800.00 per person, but costs vary according to ship, type of cabin, departure date, and other variables. If clients are disappointed when a price is quoted, provide recommendations for shorter cruises or other cost-saving alternatives. If clients act disinterested when a price is quoted, start asking qualifying questions to determine further recommendations in case an upgrade is warranted. The agent must be considerate when asking about the client's budget. Some clients may be intimidated by the question of money, others may welcome the candor, and some are not concerned at all with the cost. Below is a very simple form that a client can complete to give you a good idea of details that matter.

I would like to sail to _____. I think that a _____ day cruise is right for me. I prefer _____ (small/large/any size) ships. I would like a cruise that has _____ (many/ few activities. I would like a cruise that visits _____ many/few ports. I exercise _____ regularly/daily/infrequently. I want to go on the cruise with _____ (spouse/friend/family/group). I enjoy/like: ___ scuba ___ snorkeling ___ shopping ___ gambling ___ running ___ reading ___ cards ___ games ___ crafts ___ romantic times ___ dancing ___ movies ___ relaxing ___ swimming ___ sightseeing ___ meeting people ___ quiet times ___ sunbathing ___ aerobics ___ windsurfing ___ horseback riding ___ archaeology ___ good value for money ___ the best in all details ___ exotic, special—price doesn't matter
Other _____

A traveler's profile form is ideal for qualifying the client, not only for cruises but for all the specifics of travel needs and expectations. The figure on page 77 provides a sample.

*See "Special Needs Passengers" section in Chapter 2

TRAVELER'S PROFILE FORM

Have you been to our agency before? If not, please take a moment to fill out the form so that we may know more about your needs and be able to provide professional services to you.

Date _____

NAME _____   HOME PHONE _____

ADDRESS _____   WORK PHONE _____

CITY/STATE/ZIP _____   BEEPER _____ FAX _____

E-MAIL _____ CITIZENSHIP _____

DO YOU HAVE A VALID PASSPORT? _____   HOW DID YOU HEAR ABOUT OUR

AGENCY? _____ FRIEND _____ NEWSPAPER AD _____ YELLOW PAGES   IF OTHER,

PLEASE PROVIDE INFO _____

WHAT IS YOUR PROFESSION/BUSINESS? _____

ABOUT HOW MANY TRIPS TO YOU TAKE A YEAR? _____   ABOUT WHAT PERCENTAGE ARE

TRIPS FOR BUSINESS? _____   PLEASURE/VACATION? _____

WHICH AREAS HAVE YOU VISITED: ____ FLORIDA ____ CALIFORNIA ____ HAWAII

____ ALASKA ____ CANADA ____ CARIBBEAN ____ CENTRAL AMERICA ____ EUROPE

____ SOUTH AMERICA ____ AFRICA ____ MID EAST ____ ASIA ____ AUSTRALIA ____ PACIFIC

WHAT AREAS ARE YOU INTERESTED IN TRAVELING TO? _____

_____

DO YOU PREFER TO TRAVEL INDEPENDENTLY OR WITH A GROUP? _____

DO YOU PREFER ____ DELUXE ____ FIRST CLASS ____ STANDARD ACCOMMODATIONS?

____ guided tours ____ gourmet dining ____ good beaches ____ sightseeing ____ shopping

____ experiencing cultures ____ nightlife ____ relaxing ____ meeting people ____ events

____ sports ____ golf ____ tennis ____ diving ____ snorkeling ____ skiing

____ hiking ____ camping   OTHER _____

WHAT TOUR COMPANIES HAVE YOU USED? _____

_____ ANY COMMENTS ON THEM? _____

_____

HAVE YOU TAKEN A CRUISE? _____ IF NO, WOULD YOU LIKE TO? _____ IF YES, WHAT

SHIPS AND AREAS HAVE YOU EXPERIENCED? _____

_____

DO YOU PREFER ANY SHIPS/CRUISE LINES? _____

WHAT IS THE AVERAGE AMOUNT YOU SPEND PER PERSON ON A TRIP?

____ UNDER $1000 ____ $1000–$2000 ____ $2000–$3000 ____ $3000–$4000 ____ OVER $4000

DO YOU HAVE ANY MEDICAL CONDITIONS/ALLERGIES? _____

_____

ARE THERE ANY FREQUENT FLYER/TRAVELER PROGRAMS YOU WOULD LIKE CONSIDERED?

_____

ARE YOU A MEMBER OF ANY CLUBS/ASSOCIATIONS?   WHICH ONES? _____

SELLING TO TODAY'S CLIENTS

Today's clients are very hurried and plan their trips/vacations with little overall preparation time. They are more educated about their options as well as destinations and products. They need answers to many questions, and they are easily disappointed if an agent doesn't seem knowledgeable or act competently and professionally. Videos are a big plus in the sales process, as they can effectively provide the specifics and highlights of the cruise. Agents should review the videos ahead of time to be familiar with their contents and to make certain they are up-to-date.

Qualify clients before offering videos. The clients' reaction will depend on their expectations and wants. Videos can be misleading about cabin size. In addition, ports may be featured that are not included on a specific itinerary.

One of the most important influences is the local newspaper. Agents should bring in and become familiar with local, current advertising. Clients are also influenced by recommendations given by their friends and associates. The agent needs to make sure the clients' needs, budget, and all other considerations have been included in the selection and decision process.

Agencies should work with a select group of cruise lines, in order to meet the varying needs of consumers the group should include a product mix that contains mass market, upscale, luxury, and specialty cruises. By working with a select group, agents can maximize their product knowledge and make the agency more valuable to the cruise lines. A volume of sales provides overrides and bonuses, as well as cooperative advertising and promotions.

Agents should not quote prices from brochures. In today's marketplace, discounts are rampant. It is best to concentrate on selling the line, the ship, the itinerary, and the date (after taking the time to qualify the client). Brochures should be used to get clients involved. Agents should highlight with a marker important details or areas. This "personalizes" the brochure for clients—getting them excited and committed to the idea.

Agents should not ask clients if they can make a reservation. They can tell the clients they're calling to see if space is available on the cruise in which they are interested. If space is not available, the agent can use this as proof that cruises are popular and need to be booked as early as possible. If space is available, the agent can advise the clients to hold the space for the few days it may take to decide. The agents should ask for a deposit in two or three days (even if the option is for one week), so the clients' excitement remains strong.

When faced with advertised discount prices, agents can first check directly with the cruise line or contact the cruise line's sales representative to see if the prices advertised are indeed legitimate and how the agency can obtain the discount. If there is no possibility of matching the rate, the agent can stress to the clients that "price isn't everything"—maybe the services are not professional or reliable. If the price is through an "out-of-town" agency, emphasize the advantages of working with local agencies for easy contact and the greater risk and possible inconveniences if problems should occur with the out-of-town agency. Offer other incentives, such as a bon voyage gift or other extras.

Gifts for Cruise Clients

Agencies should establish policies for gifts provided to clients who have booked a cruise. Most agencies will not send a gift for the purchase of a three- or four-day cruise, but will provide one if a seven-day (or longer) cruise has been purchased. A formula for gifts can be "$5.00 for every $1,000.00 spent" (for example, a $25.00 gift for a $5,000.00 cruise). More expensive gifts may be involved with regular clients or repeat customers.

It is important to make sure the gift is appropriate. If the clients do not drink, don't send a bottle of champagne. Fruit baskets are not always appropriate since fruit is available at no charge on board the ships. Flower arrangements are nice, but they do not provide a lasting memory. Here are some gift ideas:

- Limousine service to and from the ship
- Bottle of champagne/wine delivered to the cabin
- Bottle of wine at dinner
- Bottles of sparkling juices
- A credit toward a bar tab
- A gift certificate for the shop on board, the beauty salon, or for on board photos
- Travel guidebooks
- A pocket/disposable camera, film
- Blank videotapes
- Compact binoculars
- A subscription to *Cruise Travel* magazine
- Certificate for a massage
- Paid shore excursion (these can be quite expensive)
- Flower leis (particularly for Hawaii cruises)
- Trip diaries, photo albums

Most important, make sure the clients know the gift is from the agency. Attach a business card to the gift order form and ask that it be included with the gift.

Major Factors that Determine the Choice and Cost of a Cruise

- SEASON—periods of high season (peak demand), shoulder season (moderate demand), and low/value season (low demand). See the box on HIGH SEASON.
- SPACE RATIO—the ratio of the size of the ship to the number of passengers.
- SHIP SERVICES AND FACILITIES—the ratio of the number of crew to the number of passengers and all the amenities offered.
- ITINERARIES—the ports of call, length of cruise.
- ACCOMMODATIONS—the types of cabins, square footage, types of beds, extras such as hair dryers, safes, phones, TVs, VCRs, and so on.
- ACTIVITIES—the casinos, shows, all types of entertainment, sports, equipment, staff-directed programs.

One of the measurements of a ship's services and classification is the estimated per diem. Per diems are approximate costs for cruise only, based on double occupancy and calculated by averaging the ship's peak and off-peak rates. *Travel Trade* magazine periodically lists the per diems of many ships, which can be used for reference. Carnival's *Holiday* ship has an estimated per diem of $210.00, while the *Sun Princess* of Princess Cruises has an estimated per diem of $300.00.

A variety of references should be on hand for the agent to refer to in the selection process. It is important for agencies to have copies of consumer references as well as industry/trade references so they can be familiar with what consumers are reading and have the extra information and more thorough detail provided by trade publications.

Personal experiences of cruise ships are very helpful, but it's almost impossible for agents to experience all the different ships and to keep current when refurbishing and other changes are made. Agents participating in ship inspections should complete a cruise ship evaluation form. This form should be circulated among the agency staff and perhaps discussed at a staff meeting. Agents may want to give evaluation forms to valued clients—as their opinions can add to resource information. A sample cruise ship evaluation form is provided later in this chapter.

High Season

In the Caribbean, high season is between Christmas and April and during the summer. Yet, there may be special offers put out when bookings are "soft." The January through April time frame targets seniors and snowbirds. The family market dominates the summer months. Remember that during high season ships will tend to be full, so not only are they more expensive, they're crowded.

Qualifying the Client

Qualifying questions include the client's budget, dates of travel, likes and dislikes, cruise and other travel experiences, destinations preferred, special needs or requirements, and so on. It takes a great deal of experience to get to know all the different cruise lines and to be able to recommend a specific and appropriate cruise to a client.

The *length of cruise* will limit the possibilities. Further research is then necessary. If an agent is trying to pick from a group of cruise ships that all offer seven-day cruises, it will be helpful to read some of the descriptions or comments in the guides/references so that the agent and client can together evaluate the possibilities. Reading the comments from the Berlitz guide provides an easy summary of the cruise experience and can highlight certain aspects that would either appeal to or disappoint the client. The *previous experiences* of the client are valuable to the selection process. If clients have sailed on a "luxury class" cruise ship, they are not likely to appreciate a "budget cruise." *First-time cruisers* might be best suited to start out with a two-, three-, or four-night cruise. Clients may have a preference for the *nationality of the crew, the size of the ship, and amenities. Prices* are the definite indicator of the type of service, atmosphere, and passengers that will be on board a ship. Some cruise ships are more relaxing than others, so *find out the atmosphere the client prefers.* The choice of *itineraries* will also influence the selection process.

The key to professional and effective cruise selling is to ask a lot of questions and make notes. Establish a bond with clients by having them complete the traveler's profile form, or complete it with them at your desk. Establish a level of communication with clients that puts them at ease. Pay attention to what the clients say and their body language. Organize the information for the clients and make certain all their questions have been fully answered to their complete satisfaction.

WHAT'S WRONG WITH THE WAY
THE AGENT RESPONDS IN THESE EXAMPLES?

CLIENT: Hi, I'm interested in a cruise.

AGENT: There's a special promotion going on right now for XYZ Cruise Lines.

_____

_____

CLIENT: My wife and I are interested in a cruise to the Caribbean.

AGENT: Well, if you want to go now, it's hurricane season.

_____

_____

CLIENT: Our family was thinking about a reunion on a cruise.

AGENT: You'll have to book more than 10 cabins to get a discount.

_____

_____

CLIENT: I really don't want to spend more than $1,000.00 on a cruise.

AGENT: There are some cheap cruises that would cost about $300.00 a person.

_____

_____

SELLING SKILLS

In addition to "qualifying the client" with the various items, the travel agent should have additional skills for selling cruises.

1. _Knowledge about the cruise products_
   Utilize training manuals; attend seminars and conferences; read brochures, industry magazines, and the consumer press; watch videos; and be familiar with cruise ships, events, and promotions. Join the Cruise Lines International Association and other professional organizations that can assist you in skills and training, and provide you with contacts and resources.

2. _Access to references and resources to answer questions and obtain information_
   Have online database information; subscribe to and purchase cruise reference books and publications; have brochures, videos, and other selling tools accessible, organized, and updated.

3. _Good research skills and communication skills to relate information_

4. *Knowledge of current promotions, special offers, and possible preferred supplier relationships*

5. *Procedural skills to reserve space, handle payments and other documentation necessary, and to provide professional services*

Key Points About Selling Cruises

Sell a "cruise," not a particular ship. If the ship the clients have requested or one you initially recommend is not available, you can try another.

Sell a category of cabins, not a specific cabin. After choosing a category, contact the cruise line for the cabins available, and then select the best one.

Explain about guarantees. If the cruise line offers a guaranteed category rate, be sure the client understands that there is a *possibility* of an upgrade—but *only* a possibility.

Get alternative dates. Try for alternatives if the selected departure is not available, so that you can offer "some good news" to the clients.

More details on sales techniques are provided in the *Sales and Marketing Techniques* manual from *The Travel Training Series,* such as the psychology of selling, listening skills, telephone courtesy, outside sales, group travel, communication and management skills.

WHICH CRUISE TO CHOOSE

In the selection process, agents will find it helpful to have an idea of the style and environment that each cruise line provides. Although ships within the specific cruise line may vary, here is a general outline of many of the cruise lines and a description of their "personality." (This information is subject to change.)

Abercrombie and Kent—Specialty cruises for mostly experienced travelers. Most activity takes place off the ships, as zodiacs allow passengers to make landfall nearly anywhere. Naturalists lead excursions for wildlife and other encounters.

American Canadian Caribbean Line—Yacht-like ships that are custom-designed for cruising inland waterways. These no-frills cruises offer excellent value and down-home charm and personal service. Recommended for travelers seeking friendship, companionship, and light adventure to unusual destinations at a slow pace.

Carnival Cruise Lines—"The most popular cruise line in the world," with a large variety of "Fun Ships" to choose from. Good value for money. Attracts repeat customers. Recommended for first-time cruisers; not recommended for sophisticated travelers who prefer luxury.

Celebrity Cruise Lines—Casually elegant and known for its excellent cuisine. Recommended for middle- to upper-income travelers; not recommended for small ship devotees.

Clipper Cruise Line—Shallow-draft, zodiac-equipped vessels offer stylish coastal cruising with a country club atmosphere. Recommended for travelers who like the cozy ambience of a country inn and experienced travelers who seek quieter and informative travel experiences.

Club Med—Sleek sailing ships offering exotic itineraries and the unique "Club Med" experience. Recommended for Francophiles and travelers who like a French ambience.

Costa Cruises—Italian spirit, superb cuisine, good service, and European ambience. Recommended for travelers who like Italian ambience, first-time cruisers, and repeat cruisers who haven't experienced the Italian-style cruising experience.

Cruise West—Combining eco-tourism with cruising, this line operates small vessels that can explore narrow inlets, fjords, and rivers. Recommended for small ship devotees, travelers looking for light adventure, and those interested in wildlife. Not recommended for gamblers, travelers who prefer discos and nightlife, and those who need to be entertained.

Crystal Cruises—A luxurious cruise experience for discriminating travelers. Typical passengers are professionals, experienced travelers, affluent, active, fashion-conscious, friendly 55 to 60-year-old couples or mature singles.

Cunard Line—Excellent service on the world renowned *Queen Elizabeth 2*. Traditional cruise experiences. In 2003 this line will offer the world's largest ocean liner, the *Queen Mary 2*.

Delta Queen Steamboat—Leisurely river cruising on paddle-wheel steamboats. Most passengers are well-traveled retirees; many are repeat passengers. Recommended for seniors, travelers interested in American history, and those who like a relaxed pace and the proximity and visibility of the shoreline that river cruises provide. Recommended for travelers who like Dixieland jazz.

Disney Cruise Line—Family-oriented mainstream cruises combined with Disney World vacations designed for all ages. Not recommended for anyone who isn't thrilled with Disney productions and parks.

Holland America Line—With a 120-year heritage of Dutch seamanship, Holland America offers premium cruise value, spacious staterooms, and impeccable service. Not recommended for party seekers, late-night trendsetters, and young singles. *Note:* There's a no tipping required policy.

Lindblad Expeditions—Passengers are well traveled, usually over age 60, and interested in travel experiences that enrich and stimulate their minds.

Norwegian Cruise Line—The official cruise line of the NFL, NBA, and Universal Studios in Florida and Hollywood. NCL has big ships, small ships, old ships, and new ships. Recommended for first-time cruisers and those with special interests related to the theme cruises offered.

Orient Lines—Cruises to exotic destinations at affordable prices.

P & O Cruises—The Peninsular and Oriental Steam Navigation Company began in the early 1800s. It is part of a huge conglomerate of companies involved in cargo shipping as well as construction and real estate. P & O Cruises and Princess Cruises are owned together.

Princess Cruises—The famous "Love Boat" fleet offers richly appointed and spacious ships. Fine dining, excellent entertainment, and good service add to the experience. It's one of the most aggressive and prosperous cruise lines, and best known for its Alaska and Caribbean presence. Recommended for modestly affluent first-time cruisers, and not recommended for swingers.

Radisson Diamond Cruise—Superior stability is afforded by the twin-hull design, along with luxury cabins, topnotch entertainment and 5-star dining. Recommended for upscale, independent, active, seasoned travelers accustomed to luxury and quality.

Regal Cruise Line—Budget-conscious travelers will enjoy first-time cruising with this line's one-, three-, four-, six-, and 10-day cruises.

Royal Caribbean International—Award-winning services, spectacular and modern ships, excellent cuisine, great entertainment and value. However, cabins are somewhat smaller. Ideal for families with several generations traveling together, as there is a diversity of shipboard activities and programs.

Royal Olympic Cruise Line—The merger of Sun Line Cruises and Epirotiki Cruises has given this line a continuation of a casually elegant atmosphere, European service, and exotic itineraries. Recommended for travelers wanting a comfortable way to visit interesting destinations.

Seabourn Cruise Line—Ultimate cruise experience for discriminating travelers. All suites and the service and cuisine are unmatched. Recommended for sophisticated travelers. Not recommended for children. No tipping allowed.

Silversea Cruises—With nearly 75% of the 155 suites having teak-decked verandahs, the style and furnishings are wonderful. Per diems average about half the charges of other deluxe cruises.

Star Clippers—Experience old-fashioned sailing on these ships that re-create 19th-century vessels. Guests can pitch the sails, help steer the ship, and learn about navigational techniques.

Windjammer Barefoot Cruises—Totally laid-back and casual cruising.

Windstar Cruises—Extraordinary four-masted ships pampering the maximum of 148 passengers with high-tech amenities and exceptional service and cuisine.

World Explorer Cruises—Cultural and educational cruise experiences (no casinos or discos).

A great tool is to create a database/indexed file of information on the ships, cruise lines, and ports of embarkation. Ships' data, such as tonnage, crew, cabins, ratios, itineraries, and so on, along with special information/hints would be invaluable—although it would need to be kept current. Transportation to the ports and parking details will also be handy. File folders with sample menus, activity sheets, shore excursions, and prices will be extremely useful for giving the ultimate details to clients.

CRUISE LINES AND CRUISE SHIPS

Note: All information is subject to change after printing.

Abercrombie & Kent
1520 Kensington Rd. Ste. 212
Oak Brook, IL 60523
(630) 954-2944 or (800) 323-7308
Fax: (630) 954-3324
<http://www.abercrombiekent.com>

Explorer
Note: Other ships may be used around the world

Cruises through inland waterways such as the Nile River, China's Yangtze River, and barge trips in France, Holland, Belgium, and England. Sailings along the Turkish coastline, and cruises to the Galapagos Islands, cruises in the South Pacific and to Antarctica are also offered.

Amazon Tours and Cruises
275 Fountainbleau Blvd. Ste 173
Miami, FL 33172
(305) 227-2266 or (800) 423-2791
Fax: (305) 227-1880
<http://www.amazontours.net>

MV Rio Amazonas
MV Arca
MV Amazon Explorer
MV Delfin
MV Marcelita

Amazon River cruises and tours that include nature expeditions.

American Canadian Caribbean Line
P.O. Box 368
Warren, RI 02885
(401) 247-0955 or (800) 556-7450
Fax: (401) 247-2350
<http://www.accl-smallships.com>

MV Grande Caribe
MV Niagara Prince
MV Grande Mariner

Yacht-style cruising through the eastern inland waterways of the United States and Canada, along the Eastern Seaboard of the United States, around Florida and the Caribbean, Central and South America.

American West Steamboat Company
2101 4th Avenue, Suite 1150
Seattle, WA 98121
(206) 292-9606 or (800) 434-1232
Fax: (206) 340-0975
<http://www.columbiarivercruise.com>

Queen of the West
Empress of the North

Cruise programs from two to seven days March through December from Portland, Oregon, on the Columbia, Snake, and Willamette rivers.

Blackbeard Cruises
P.O. Box 661091
Miami, FL 33266
(305) 888-1226 or (800) 327-9600
Fax: (305) 884-4214
<http://www.blackbeard-cruises.com>

SV Morning Star
SV Pirate's Lady
SV Sea Explorer
SV Cat Ppalu

Sailing vessels designed for fishing and scuba diving vacations in the Bahamas and the Caribbean. Singles comprise about 60% of the clientele.

Carnival Cruise Line
3655 NW 87th Ave.
Miami, FL 33178-2428
(305) 599-2600 or (800) 327-9501
Fax: (305) 471-4740
<http://www.carnival.com>

Celebration, Holiday, Jubilee,
Elation, Fantasy, Sensation, Ecstasy,
Imagination, Fascination,
Inspiration, Destiny, Paradise,
Triumph, Victory, Spirit, Pride,
Conquest, Legend, Glory (2003),
Miracle (2004), *Valor* (2004)

Carnival cruise programs feature three to seven day itineraries to the Bahamas, the Caribbean, the Mexican Riviera, and Alaska. The *Paradise* is a non-smoking ship.

Celebrity Cruises
1050 Caribbean Way
Miami, FL 33126
(305) 539-6000 or (800) 437-3111
Fax (800) RCCL FAX
<http://www.celebrity-cruises.com>

Century, Horizon, Zenith, Galaxy,
Mercury, Millennium, Infinity,
Summit, Constellation

Seven- to twelve-day cruises to the eastern and western Caribbean, Bermuda, Alaska, Europe, and the Mediterranean. A 12- to 14-night itinerary in South America on the *Mercury* is also available.

Clipper Cruise Line
11969 West Line Industrial Drive
St. Louis, MO 63146
(814) 655-6700 or (800) 325-0010
Fax: (814) 655-6670
<http://www.clippercruise.com>

Nantucket Clipper
Yorktown Clipper
Clipper Adventurer
Clipper Odyssey

This cruise line's fleet sails both coasts of North America and the intracoastal waterway and spends the winter season in the Caribbean. The *Clipper Adventurer* sails in Europe and to Antarctica, as well as to Greenland. The *Clipper Odyssey* sails to Australia and New Zealand, Japan and Indonesia. It also goes to Russia.

Club Med Cruises
75 Valencia Ave. 9th Floor
Coral Gables, FL 33134
(305) 925-9000 or (800) 258-2633
Fax: (305) 443-0562
<http://www.clubmed.com>

Club Med 2

One-week cruises in the Caribbean and three to 10-day cruises in the Mediterranean.

Costa Cruise Lines
Venture Corp. Center, Suite 200
200 South Park Road
Hollywood, FL 33021
(954) 266-5600 or (800) 462-6782
Fax: (954) 266-2100
<http://www. costacruises.com>

Costa Allegra, Costa Classica,
Costa-Romantica, Costa Victoria,
Costa Atlantica, Costa Tropicale,
Costa Europa, Costa Mediterranea
(2003), *Costa Fortuna* (2003)
Costa Magica (2004)

Cruises to destinations in the Caribbean, Alaska, Mediterranean, Europe, and the Black Sea. Transatlantic cruises are also offered. This Italian-style cruising company is celebrating services for more than 50 years.

Cruise West
2401 4th Ave. Ste. 700
Seattle, WA 98121
(206) 441-8687 or (800) 426-7702
Fax: (206) 441-4757
<http://www.cruisewest.com>

Spirit of Alaska
Spirit of Discovery
Spirit of Columbia
Spirit of '98
Sheltered Seas, Spirit of Oceanus
Spirit of Endeavor
Pacific Explorer

Sightseeing excursion-type vessels visit wilderness areas and inland waterways in Alaska, in British Columbia, and on the Columbia River, including Vancouver Island, the San Juan Islands, and Puget Sound. Sightseeing vessels also visit the wine country out of San Francisco, the Sea of Cortez in Mexico, and Central America.

Crystal Cruises
2049 Century Park East, Ste. 1400
Los Angeles, CA 90067
(310) 785-9300 or (800) 446-6620
Fax: (310) 785-0011
<http://www.crystalcruises.com>

Crystal Harmony
Crystal Symphony
Crystal Serenity (2003)

Six- to 26-day cruises in Europe, the Pacific, and the Orient, plus transcanal cruises.

Cunard Line
6100 Blue Lagoon Dr. Ste. 400
Miami, FL 33126
(305) 463-3000 or (800) 5-CUNARD
Fax: (305) 463-3038
<http://www.cunardline.com>

Queen Elizabeth 2
Caronia
Queen Mary 2 (2003)

Cruises from two to 109 days to the Caribbean, Europe, and the Mediterranean.

Delta Queen Steamboat Company
1380 Robin St. Wharf Port of New Orleans Place
New Orleans, LA 70130-1890
(504) 586-0631 or (800) 543-1949
Fax: (504) 585-0630
<http://www.deltaqueen.com>

Mississippi Queen
Delta Queen
American Queen

Cruises on these steamboats range from three to 14 days and cruise on the Mississippi, Arkansas, and Ohio rivers.

DFDS SeaEurope Holidays
6555 NW 9th Ave., Ste. 207
Ft. Lauderdale, FL 33309
(954) 491-7909 or (800) 533-3755
Fax: (954) 491-7958
<http://www.dfdsseaways.com>
<http://www.seaeurope.com>

Crown of Scandinavia
Dana Anglia,
Prince of Scandinavia
Princess of Scandinavia
Queen of Scandinavia
Admiral of Scandinavia
Pearl of Scandinavia

Point-to-point overnight cruises in northern Europe.

Discovery Cruises
1775 NW 70th Ave.
Miami, FL 33126
(305) 597-0336 or (800) 866-8687
Fax: (305) 436-9712
<http://www.discoverycruiseline.com>

Discovery Sun

One-day cruises to Freeport, Bahamas—seven days a week with hotel packages for stopovers.

Disney Cruise Line
210 Celebration Place, Ste. 400
Celebration, FL 34747
(407) 566-3500, (800) 511-1333
Fax: (407) 939-3751
<http://www.disneycruise.com>

Disney Magi
Disney Wonder

Three- to four-day cruises to the Caribbean, seven-night land and sea cruises. Also, a seven-night cruise to the eastern Caribbean.

Fred Olsen Cruise Lines/The Cruise Broker//Kristina Cruises
P.O. Box 342
New York, NY 10014
(212) 352-8854 or (800) 688-3876
Fax: (212) 504-8057
<http://www.thecruisebroker.net>

MS Braemar
Kristina Regina
Black Watch
Black Prince

Five to 10-day cruises of the Baltic Sea, Scotland, and Norway.

First European Cruises
95 Madison Ave., Ste. 609
New York, NY 10016
(212) 779-7168 or (888) 983-8767
Fax (212) 779-0948
<http://www.first-european.com>

Azur
Bolero
Mistral
Flamenco, European Vision
European Stars
yet-to-be-named (2003)

Seven-, 10-, and 17-night cruises in the Mediterranean, Europe, Middle East, Africa, Caribbean, and Transatlantic.

French Country Waterways
P.O. Box 2195
Duxbury, MA 02331
(781) 934-2454 or (800) 222-1236
Fax: (781) 934-9048
<http://www.fcwl.com>

*Horizon II, Esprit, Nenuphar,
Liberte, Princess*

French barge cruises generally operated from April to October.

Galapagos Inc.
7800 Red Rd., Ste. 112
South Miami, FL 33143
(305) 665-0841 or (800) 327-9854
Fax: (305) 661-1457
<http://www.galapagoscruises.net>

Galapagos Explorer II

Three-, four-, and seven-day cruises of the Galapagos Islands.

Galapagos Network
6303 Blue Lagoon Dr. Ste 140
Miami, FL 33126
(305) 262-6264 or (800) 633-7972
Fax: (305) 262-9609
<http://www.eclventura.com>

*MY Eric
MY Flamingo
MY Letty
MV Corinthian
MY Sky Dancer*

Three-, four-, and seven-day cruises of the Galapagos Islands.

Globalquest
185 Willis Ave., 2nd Floor
Mineola, NY 11501
(516) 739-3690 or (800) 221-3254
Fax: (516) 739-8022
<http://www.globalquest.com>

*Peter the Great
Amadeus
Amadeus II
Amadeus Classic
Ambassador
Eclipse*

River cruises, cruises in Europe, Black Sea, Russia, Seychelles, South America, the Galapagos, Antarctica, North Pole, and Arctic Ocean.

Great Lakes Cruise Company
3300 Washtenaw Avenue, Ste. 230
Ann Arbor, MI 48104
(734) 677-0900 or (888) 891-0203
Fax (734) 677-3128
<http://www.greatlakescruising.com>

*Le Levant
MV Columbus
MV Georgian Clipper*

Voyages of discovery on North America's inland seas.

Holland America Line
300 Elliott Ave. W.
Seattle, WA 98119
(206) 281-3535 or (800) 426-0327
Fax: (206) 281-0627
<http://www.hollandamerica.com>

MS Amsterdam
MS Noordam
MS Rotterdam, MS Ryndam,
MS Maasdam
MS Statendam, MS Veendam,
MS Volendam, MS Zaandam
MS Prinsendan
MS Zuiderdam
MS Oosterdam (2003)
ships yet-to-be-named 2004-2006

Cruise programs from seven to 99 days visiting destinations in the Caribbean, Alaska, the Orient, Europe, South America, the Pacific, eastern Canada and the Panama Canal, plus a world cruise.

JFO Cruise Service Corp./KD River Cruises of Europe
2500 Westchester Ave.
Purchase, NY 10577
(914) 696-3600 or (800) 346-6525 (east)
Fax: (914) 696-0833
<http://www.rivercruises.com>

Arlene, Clara Schumann,
Normandie, Deutschland,
Heinrich Heine, Theodore
Fontaine, Helvetia, Britannia

River cruises on the Rhine, Moselle, and Main rivers, also the Elbe, Seine, Rhine Saone, and Danube rivers.

Linblad Expeditions
720 5th Ave., 6th Floor
New York, NY 10019
(212) 765-7740 or (800) 762-0003
Fax: (212) 265-3770
<http://www.expeditions.com>

Polaris
Sea Bird
Sea Lion
Endeavour

This company caters to small groups (10 to 100 passengers) who are interested in subjects such as ornithology, marine biology, geology, culture, and history. Destinations include ports in Alaska, along the Columbia and Snake rivers, ports of Europe, Central and South America.

Mediterranean Shipping Cruises
420 Fifth Ave.
New York, NY 10018
(212) 764-4800 or (800) 666-9333
Fax (212) 764-1486
<http://www.msccruisesusa.com>

Melody
Rhapsody
Monterey
Symphony (not marketed
in United States)

Destinations include the Caribbean, Mediterranean, South America, South Africa, and Transatlantic.

Navigant Travel/Inland Voyages
112 Prospect St.
Stamford, CT 06901
(203) 978-5010 or (800) 786-5311
Fax: (203) 978-5027

Luciole

Six-day cruises on the inland waterways of the Burgundy region of France, departing April through October.

Nabila Tours and Cruises
605 Market St., Ste. 507
San Francisco, CA 94105
(415) 979-0160 or (800) 443-NILE
Fax: (415) 979-0163
<http://www.nabilatours.com>

Queen of Sheba
Ramses—King of the Nile
King of Thebes
Queen of the Nile
Al Nabilatan
Queen of Abu Simbel

Three- and four-night Nile River cruises and three- and four-night cruises on Lake Nasser.

Nekton Diving Cruises
520 SE 32nd St.
Ft. Lauderdale, FL 33316
(954) 463-9324 or (800) 899-6753
Fax: (954) 463-8938
<http://www.nektoncruises.com>

Nekton Pilot
Nekton Rorqual

Saturday to Saturday cruises of Bahamian dive sites, from Ft. Lauderdale, and during the winter months cruises out of Great Exuma and Belize City.

Norwegian Coastal Voyages Inc./Bergen Line Services
405 Park Ave.
New York, NY 10022
(212) 319-1300 or (800)323-7436
Fax: (212) 319-1390
<http://www.coastalvoyage.com>

Richard With, Polarlys,
Nordkapp, Nordlys, Midnatsol,
Narvik, Vesteraalen, Kong Harald,
Nordnorge, Lofoten,
Harald Jarl, Finnmarken,
Trollfjord

Cruising itineraries along the west coast of Norway. This company also represents Silja Line in the United States for the operations of some of the ships in the Baltic Sea and Scandinavian area.

Norwegian Cruise Line
7665 Corporate Center Dr.
Miami, FL 33126
(305) 436-0866 or (800) 327-7030
Fax: (305) 436-4130
<http://www.ncl.com>

Norway
Norwegian Wind
Norwegian Sea
Norwegian Dream
Norwegian Majesty
Norwegian Sun
Norwegian Sky
Norwegian Star
Norwegian Dawn

Cruises to the Bahamas, Caribbean, Bermuda, Mexico, Hawaii, Alaska, South America, Europe, and Australia.

Orient Lines
1510 SE 17th St., Ste. 300
Ft. Lauderdale, FL 33316
(954) 527-6660 or (800) 333-7300
Fax: (954) 527-6657
<http://www.orientlines.com>

Marco Polo
Crown Odyssey

Cruise programs from seven to 25 days with destinations in Southeast Asia, New Zealand, Australia, Kenya, South Africa, the Indian Ocean, India, Antarctica, the Mediterranean, and Egypt.

Palm Beach Casino Line
77 E. Port Rd.
Riviera Beach, FL 33404
(407) 845-2101 or (800) 841-7447
Fax: (407) 845-2188
<http://www.pbcasino.com>

Palm Beach Princess

Twice-daily cruises, seven days a week for gambling and entertainment.

P & O Cruises (several worldwide headquarters)
<http://www.pocruises.com>

Victoria, Arcadia, Oriana,
Minerva, Aurora

Peter Dielmann Cruises
1800 Diagonal Rd., Ste. 170
Alexandria, VA 22314
(800) 348-8287 or (703) 549-1741
Fax (703) 549-7924
<http://www.deilmann-cruises.com>

Lili Marleen, Deutschland,
Prussian Princess, Mozart, Princesse
de Provence, Konigstein, Katharina,
Dresden, Danube Princess, Cezanne,
Casanova, Fredric Chopin

A fleet of river ships sailing on the inland waterways of Europe as well as two oceangoing vessels.

Princess Cruises
24844 Avenue
Rockefeller
Santa Clarita, CA 91355
(800) 421-0522
Fax: (661) 284-4745
<http://www.princesscruises.com>

Royal Princess, Regal Princess,
Sea Princess, Sun Princess,
Dawn Princess, Ocean Princess,
Grand Princess, Golden Princess,
Star Princess, Coral Princess,
Diamond Princess (2003),
Island Princess (2003),
Sapphire Princess (2004)

Cruise programs from three to 105 days to destinations in the Caribbean, Mexico, Alaska, the South Pacific, Hawaii and Tahiti, the Orient, Europe, India, the Holy Land, South America and the Amazon River, Canada and New England, Africa, and the Panama Canal.

Radisson Seven Seas Cruises
600 Corporate Dr.
Ft. Lauderdale, FL 33334
(402) 501-5000 (800) 285-1835
Fax: (402) 431-5599
<http://www.rssc.com>

Radisson Diamond
Hanseatic (seasonal)
Song of Flower
Seven Seas Navigator
Paul Gaugin
Seven Seas Mariner
Seven Seas Voyager

The *Radisson Diamond* is a twin-hulled ship offering three- to 10-day cruises of the Caribbean, transcanal, transatlantic, and the Mediterranean. The *Hanseatic* features 11-day cruises to Antartica (seasonal). The *Paul Gaugin* sails Tahiti year-round. Contact the line for other itineraries.

Regal China Cruises
57 West 38th St.
New York, NY 10018
(212) 768-3388 or (800) 808-3388
Fax (212) 768-4939
<http://www.regalchinacruises.com>

Princess Elaine
Princess Sheena
Princess Jeannie

The only five-star Western-managed cruise line in China with sailings on the Yangtze River.

Regal Cruise Line
300 Regal Cruise Way
Palmetto, FL 34221
(941) 721-7300 or (800) 270-SAIL
Fax: (941) 723-0900
<http://www.regalcruises.com>

Regal Empress

Four-, five-, and six-day cruises to Key West and Caribbean, 10-night cruises to the Panama Canal, and one-night party cruises.

RiverBarge Excursion Lines, Inc.
201 Opelousas Ave.
New Orleans, LA 70114
(504) 365-0022 or (888) 456-2206
Fax (504) 365-0000
<http://www.riverbarge.com>

River Explorer

The only barging experience in America, traveling on the Mississippi, Ohio, and other American rivers and inland waterways.

Royal Caribbean International
1050 Caribbean Way
Miami, FL 33132
(305) 539-6000 or (800) 327-6700
Fax: (800) 722-5329
<http://www.royalcaribbean.com>

Legend of the Seas
Monarch of the Seas
Majesty of the Seas
Sovereign of the Seas
Nordic Empress
Splendour of the Seas
Grandeur of the Seas
Rhapsody of the Seas
Explorer of the Seas, Voyager
of the Seas, Enchantment of the Seas
Vision of the Seas
Radiance of the Seas
Adventure of the Seas
Brilliance of the Seas
Navigator of the Sea (2003)
Serenade of the Seas (2003)
Mariner of the Seas (2003)
Jewel of the Seas (2004)

Cruises to every area of the world.

Royal Olympic Cruises
805 3rd Ave., 18th Fl.
New York, NY 10022
(212) 688-7555 or (800) 872-6400
Fax: (212) 688-2304
<http://www.royalolympiccruises.com>

Stella Solaris
Odysseus, Triton
Olympic Voyager
Olympic Countess
World Renaissance
Olympic Explorer

Cruise programs from three to 58 days in the Caribbean, Mediterranean, South America, Amazon River, Panama Canal, Greek Islands, and more.

St. Lawrence Cruise Lines
253 Ontario St.
Kingston, ONT. K7L 2Z4 CANADA
(613) 549-8091 or (800) 267-7868
Fax: (613) 549-8410
<http://www.stlawrencecruiselines.com>

Canadian Empress

Five- and six-night cruises of the St. Lawrence and Ottawa rivers.

Seabourn Cruise Line
6100 Blue Lagoon Dr. Ste. 400
Miami, FL 33126.
(305) 463-3000 or (800) 929-9595
Fax: (305) 463-3010
<http://www.seabourn.com>

Seabourn Pride
Seabourn Legend
Seabourn Spirit

Top-of-the-line luxury cruises on worldwide itineraries.

Silversea Cruises
110 E. Broward Blvd.
Ft. Lauderdale, FL 33301
(954) 522-4477 or (800) 722-6655
Fax: (954) 522-4499
<http://www.silversea.com>

Silver Cloud
Silver Wind
Silver Shadow
Silver Whisper

Luxurious cruises on worldwide itineraries.

Star Clippers
4101 Salzedo Ave.
Coral Gables, FL 33146
(305) 442-0550 or (800) 442-0551
Fax: (305) 442-1611
<http://www.starclippers.com>

Star Clipper
Star Flyer
Royal Clipper

Seven- to 30-day cruises to the Caribbean, the Mediterranean, and transatlantic.

Uniworld
17323 Ventura Blvd.
Encino, CA 91316
(800) 733-7820
<http://www.uniworldcruises.com>

Amadeus II
Douro Prince
Rhone Princess
River Princess
River Empress
River Queen
Seine Princess
Swiss Pearl
Victor Hugo
Swiss Venice
Litvinov
Tolstoy

Victoria Cruises
57-08 39th Ave.
Woodside, NY 11377
(212) 818-1680 or (800) 348-8084
Fax: (212) 818-9889
<http://www.victoriacruises.com>

Victoria I
Victoria II
Victoria III
Victoria V
Victoria VII
Victoria Princess
Victoria Pearl, Victoria Blue Whale
Victoria Rose
Victoria Empress
Victoria Prince

Three- and four-day cruises on the Yangtze River in China.

Viking River Cruises
21820 Burbank Blvd.
Woodland Hills, CA 91367
(818) 227-1234 or (800) 785-5765
Fax (818) 227-1231
<http://www.vikingrivercruises.com>

Viking Danube
Viking Pride
Viking Spirit
Viking Europe
Clara Schumann
Viking Burgundy
Viking Normandy
Venezia, Viking Kirov
Viking Pakhomov

European river cruises from nine to 16 days.

Windjammer Barefoot Cruises
P.O. Box 190120
Miami Beach, FL 33119-0120
(305) 672-6453 or (800) 327-2601
Fax: (305) 674-1219
<http://www. windjammer.com>

Amazing Grace
Flying Cloud
Mandalay
Legacy
Polynesia
Yankee Clipper

Four- to 13-day cruises to the Bahamas and the Caribbean on sailing ships.

Windstar Cruises
300 Elliott Ave. W.
Seattle, WA 98119
(206) 281-3535 or (800) 258-7245
Fax: (206) 281-0627
<http://www.windstarcruises.com>

Wind Song
Wind Spirit
Wind Star
Wind Surf

Seven-day cruises to the Caribbean and the Mediterranean, a few 14-day repositioning cruises, 10-day cruises in New Zealand.

World Explorer Cruises
555 Montgomery St., Ste. 1400
San Francisco, CA 94111-2544
(415) 820-9200 or (800) 854-3835
Fax: (415) 820-9292
<http://www.wecruise.com>

SS Universe Explorer

14-night educational cruises to Alaska.

Worldwide Travel & Cruise Associates
150 S. University Dr. , Ste. E
Plantation, FL 33324
(954) 452-8800 or (800) 881-8484
Fax: (954) 452-8884
<http://www.cruiseco.com>

Cezanne
Le Ponant
Le Levant
Panorama
Meanderer

European river cruises and cruises to the Mediterranean, Aegean, and Caribbean seas.

In addition, here are some companies that sell small-ship cruises

Lindblad Expeditions
720 5th Ave.
New York, NY 10019
(212) 765-7740 or (800) 397-3348
<http://www.lindbladexpeditions.com>

Adventure Center
1311 63rd St.
Emeryville, CA 94608
(800) 227-8747
<http://www.adventurecenter.com>

Zegraham Expeditions
192 Nickerson St., #200
Seattle, WA 98109
(206) 285-4000 or (800) 628-8747
<http://www.zeco.com>

Mountain Travel Sobek
6420 Fairmont Ave.
El Cerrito, CA 94530
(510) 527-8105
<http://www.mtsobek.com>

Quark Expeditions
980 Post Rd.
Darien, CT 06820
(203) 656-0499 or (800) 356-5699
<http://www.quarkexpeditions.com>

CHAPTER 5, TEST 1

Using the listing of cruise lines and ships, answer the following questions.

1. The *Spirit of Columbia* and the *Spirit of Discovery* are two ships operated by _____. _____.

2. Costa Cruise Lines has been operating for ____ years.

3. Cruises on the *Marco Polo* are operated by _____.

4. Crystal Cruises is headquartered in Los Angeles, California. True or False. _____

5. American Canadian Caribbean Line has the following vessels: _____ _____

6. Club Med operates _____ ships.

7. Victoria Cruises features cruises on the _____ River.

8. Name six Carnival Cruise Line ships _____ _____

9. The *Legacy* and the *Polynesia* are operated by _____.

10. Nabila Tours and Cruises is headquartered in _____.

11. _____Cruise Line operates twice-daily cruises from West Palm Beach.

12. Costa Cruises operates _____ ships at the present time.

13. The *Silver Cloud* and the *Silver Wind* are operated by which cruise line? _____

14. Palm Beach Casino Line has one ship, the _____.

15. The *Ryndam* and the *Maasdam* are two ships operated by _____.

16. Crystal Cruises operates two ships, the _____and the _____

_____.

17. The *Disney Magic* and the *Disney* _____are Disney Cruise Line ships.

18. Peter Dielmann Cruises operates the *Lili Marleen.* True or False _____

19. *Zenith, Horizon, Century, Millennium*—which cruise line features these ships? _____

20. Name four ships operated by Norwegian Cruise Line. _____

_____

21. Galapagos Network and Galapagos, Inc. are both located in Miami/South Miami, Florida.
True or False _____

22. A twin-hulled ship offering three- to 10-day cruises of the Caribbean and other world areas is the

_____.

23. Nekton Diving Cruises features diving cruises in the Cayman Islands. True or False _____

24. St. Lawrence Cruise Lines has the one ship, the _____.

25. Wind Star Cruises features four ships. Name them. _____

_____

UPDATE   **UPDATE**   **UPDATE**   **UPDATE**

WHAT HAPPENED TO THE SHIPS FROM PREMIER CRUISE LINE, WHICH CEASED OPERA-TIONS IN SEPTEMBER 2000? You will have had to keep up with cruise news. Use this box to iden-tify any new cruise line(s) and renamed ships _____

_____

_____

_____

BASIC STEPS IN SELLING CRUISES

Selling cruises, agent-client discussions, and subsequent recommendations vary tremendously, but a brief outline of selling a cruise is provided here.

1. The client comes in requesting brochures or information on a cruise, or clients call about a cruise.

2. Ask possible dates and length of the cruise. Provide suggestions if dates are flexible. Qualify client for which lines, ships, and itineraries would be suitable. Contact some cruise lines for availability.

3. If a specific line or ship is requested, go over the information. If not, select two or three cruise ships, based on the factors discussed.

4. Complete a reservation/inquiry form (a sample is on page 125) with all the necessary information. Some agencies have a software program for inputting this data.

5. If clients need to think it over, try to encourage a booking to hold the space temporarily. Most lines will hold a cabin or category rate with an "option date"—a date by which a payment is due or the reservations are cancelled.

6. Assure clients of your interest in assisting them with this trip opportunity and in answering any questions they have. Review the specific cruise details. Give a brochure with pertinent information highlighted or send the applicable details. Give your business card or name for contact, and thank them for calling/coming in.

7. Call clients about the request or follow up on the "temporary reservation" and any deposit or payment requirements.

8. At the time of deposit payment, cover details of the final payment deadline, when tickets will be processed, cancellation penalties, insurance, flight schedules, airfare, or other details.

9. Between the deposit and final payment dates, keep in touch with the client and provide additional helpful information such as maps, destination information, shore excursions (with possible pre-booking, and so on).

10. When final payment is made, go over questions, indicate when documents will be ready/mailed, provide any special "trip hints" or advice, and go over embarkation and return specifics.

11. A follow-up letter or phone call a week or two after the clients return provides valuable feedback and possible subsequent reservations.

Pricing—Cruise Only

Typically the pricing of cruises involves guarantees, early booking discounts, specials, and promotions. A guarantee is a rate that is confirmed but subject to possible upgrade if better category space becomes available later. Guarantees are usually a good deal as the chances are a better cabin will be assigned. Other specials and promotions can involve group rates, senior citizen discounts, regional area promotions (certain states, etc.), and other specifics. In addition, there may be overrides or bonuses from designated cruise lines, from membership in a consortium/association, or from a volume of sales. The cruise-only rate may or may not include port charges.

TOTAL CABIN RATE = Cabin rate per person × 2 (or single occupancy charges)
and, if applicable, add third/fourth person rate

*TOTAL CRUISE COST = TOTAL CABIN RATE + PORT CHARGES (if separate) + ADDITIONAL
SUPPLEMENTS, INSURANCE, PRE/ POST TOUR OPTIONS, ETC.*

COMMISSION = TOTAL CABIN RATE and ANY OTHER COMMISSIONABLE ITEMS
× % OF COMMISSION

Port charges not usually commissionable.

Pricing—Air/Sea

Most air/sea programs include round-trip air transportation between the passengers' origin and port of embarkation, plus transportation between the airport and the ship. The cruise line makes the flight schedule and ground transportation arrangements. From certain cities, the air/sea program provides complimentary hotel accommodations the night before the cruise because of flight schedules. There may be air deviations allowed, as explained previously.

TOTAL CABIN RATE = Cabin rate per person x 2 (or single occupancy charges)
and, if applicable, add third/fourth person rate

*TOTAL CRUISE COST = TOTAL CABIN RATE (after any deductions) + PORT CHARGES
(if separate) + AIR/SEA PROGRAM + ADDITIONAL SUPPLEMENTS,
PRE/POST ADD-ONS, INSURANCE, ETC.*

COMMISSION = TOTAL CABIN RATE and ANY OTHER COMMISSIONABLE ITEMS
× % OF COMMISSION

Port charges not usually commissionable.

Note: There may be overrides or bonus commissions from preferred cruise lines, based on the volume of sales, from promotions, or through memberships in consortiums/associations. ALTHOUGH BROCHURE RATE PRICING MAY NOT BE SO COMMON, USEFUL EXERCISES TO PRACTICE PRICING CRUISES FOLLOW.

MV SEAWORTHY

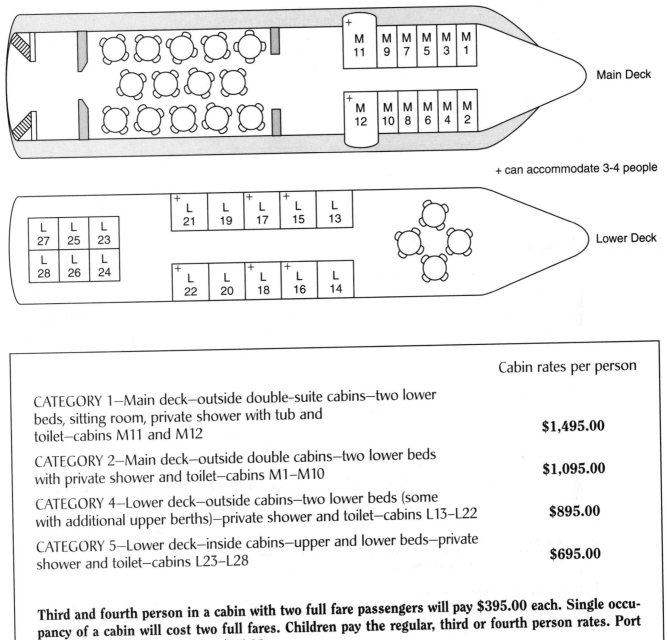

Main Deck

+ can accommodate 3-4 people

Lower Deck

	Cabin rates per person
CATEGORY 1—Main deck—outside double-suite cabins—two lower beds, sitting room, private shower with tub and toilet—cabins M11 and M12	**$1,495.00**
CATEGORY 2—Main deck—outside double cabins—two lower beds with private shower and toilet—cabins M1–M10	**$1,095.00**
CATEGORY 4—Lower deck—outside cabins—two lower beds (some with additional upper berths)—private shower and toilet—cabins L13–L22	**$895.00**
CATEGORY 5—Lower deck—inside cabins—upper and lower beds—private shower and toilet—cabins L23–L28	**$695.00**

Third and fourth person in a cabin with two full fare passengers will pay $395.00 each. Single occupancy of a cabin will cost two full fares. Children pay the regular, third or fourth person rates. Port charges are additional and are $85.00 per person.

CHAPTER 5, TEST 2

Using the sample deck plan and prices, answer the following:

1. What is the cabin rate for cabin M11? _____ per person.

2. What is the total cruise cost (include port charges) for that cabin if it was reserved for three passengers? _____

3. What is the total commission earned on that booking, using a 10% commission? _____

4. Give the cost figures for cabin M8, occupied by a party of two.

    TOTAL CABIN RATE _____ TOTAL PORT CHARGES _____

    TOTAL CRUISE COST _____ Commission (10%) _____

5. How much would a cruise for a single in cabin L23 cost? _____

MV SEAWORTHY

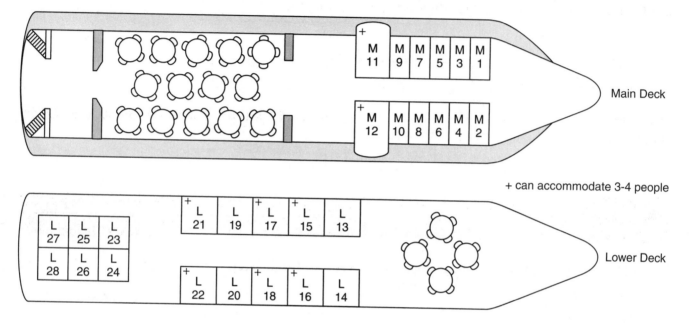

Main Deck

+ can accommodate 3-4 people

Lower Deck

	Cabin rates per person
CATEGORY 1—Main deck—outside double-suite cabins—two lower beds, sitting room, private shower with tub and toilet—cabins M11 and M12	**$1,495.00**
CATEGORY 2—Main deck—outside double cabins—two lower beds with private shower and toilet—cabins M1–M10	**$1,095.00**
CATEGORY 4—Lower deck—outside cabins—two lower beds (some with additional upper berths)—private shower and toilet—cabins L13–L22	**$895.00**
CATEGORY 5—Lower deck—inside cabins—upper and lower beds—private shower and toilet—cabins L23–L28	**$695.00**

Third and fourth person in a cabin with two full fare passengers will pay $395.00 each. Single occupancy of a cabin will cost two full fares. Children pay the regular, third or fourth person rates. Port charges are additional and are $85.00 per person.

CHAPTER 5, TEST 3

Using the sample deck plan and prices, answer the following:

1. What is the total cabin rate for cabin L25 for two people? _____

2. What is the total cruise cost for that cabin? _____

3. How much is the commission, based on 10% (refer to #1–2)? _____

4. The total cruise cost for a party of three in cabin L17 would be _____

5. Give the following figures for cabin L18 for four people:

   TOTAL CABIN RATE _____ TOTAL PORT CHARGES _____

   TOTAL CRUISE COST _____ Commission (10%) _____

Here is another pricing exercise—for a cruise with airfare included free (from New York) or special add-ons for the air from certain cities. No deck plan is provided.

OCEANIC VOYAGER III—CRUISES OF EUROPE

(Prices include round-trip air fare from New York)

CABIN CATEGORY	TYPE OF CABIN	DECK	Spring Cruise 14 days	Fall Cruise 12 days
A	Outside deluxe cabin two lowers	Riviera Promenade	$4,295	$3,995
B	Outside superior cabin two lowers	Lido Riviera	$3,845	$3,295
C	Outside superior cabin two lowers	Riviera Pacific	$3,450	$3,100
D	Outside cabin two lowers	Pacific Islander	$3,275	$2,995
E	Inside cabin two lowers	Pacific Islander	$2,895	$2,495
F	Inside cabin two lowers	Islander	$2,695	$2,250
G	Inside cabin upper and lower	Islander various	$2,295	$1,995

Rates are per person, based on double occupancy. Single occupancy add 50% supplement, except for category A cabin, add 100%. Third and fourth passengers pay minimum rate. Port charges are $135.00 for the spring cruise and $100.00 for the fall cruise.

FREE AIR FARE OR LOW ADD-ON FARES AVAILABLE—Your air fare round-trip from New York is free, and the following low add-on fares are available for other cities. If you would like extra days in Europe, the outbound and return flight can be booked for almost any dates.

U.S. CITY	ADD-ON	U.S. CITY	ADD-ON
Atlanta	$149	Orlando	$129
Boston	$99	Philadelphia	$99
Chicago	$199	Phoenix	$329
Dallas	$299	San Francisco	$429
Houston	$299	Seattle	$499
Los Angeles	$399	Tampa	$129
Miami	$99	Washington, DC	$99

CHAPTER 5, TEST 4

Using the sample prices, answer the following questions:

1. Give the total cost of a fall cruise for two passengers in a category E cabin, and using the add-on from Atlanta. _____

2. The cabin rate for a spring cruise in category C is _____ per person. If a party of three is booked (with free air from New York), what would be the total cost? _____ What is the per person cost?

3. Total cost for a fall cruise for two passengers in a category F cabin, using the add-on from Orlando is _____

Reading Brochures

In order to prepare for selling cruises, you should familiarize yourself with cruise brochures. Agents can use a binder and have reference copies of brochures that highlight specifics in pricing, booking procedures, payments, and so on. Most of the important information for the agent will be located at the back of the brochure. The front part will entice the clients with descriptions and photos of ship amenities, the food, entertainment, ports of call, and so on. Agents must go over the details of the cruise brochure carefully with clients, circling information, highlighting important points, personalizing it for the clients. When looking at the itineraries, know that when a ship arrives at a port at 8:00 A.M. for example, it doesn't mean passengers get to disembark at that time, as the ship will have to clear customs and other legalities.

Since brochures may not be available and change frequently, the following exercises are optional and the answers are not provided in the answer key.

Using a Royal Caribbean Cruise Line brochure

1. Price cabin 317 on the *Nordic Empress,* the last week in January, two adults.

   TOTAL CRUISE COST_____ TOTAL DEPOSIT REQUIRED $_____

   The FINAL PAYMENT would be $_____.

2. Price the *Sovereign of the Seas* for cabin D535 on a cruise the second week in January, for two adults.

   TOTAL CRUISE COST_____ DEPOSIT OF $_____

   FINAL PAYMENT = $_____

   COMMISSION EARNED (BASED ON 10%) = _____

3. At what time does embarkation begin in Miami? _____

4. Give two cabin numbers on the "A" deck of the *Sovereign of the Seas* that the two lower beds can be combined to form a queen-size bed. _____

5. Name the decks of the *Sovereign of the Seas* on which the following are found:

   Gymnasium _____

   Gift shops _____

   Beauty salon _____

   Casino royale _____

Using a Carnival Cruise Line Brochure:

1. Price cabin U188 on the *Jubilee,* sailing the first week in June, two adults.

   TOTAL CRUISE COST _____ DEPOSIT REQUIRED _____

   FINAL PAYMENT = _____

   TOTAL COMMISSION (BASED ON 10%) = _____

2. On what deck of the *Celebration* is the cinema located? _____

3. On what deck of the *Elation* is the spa and gymnasium located?

4. The ports on the itinerary of the four-day western Caribbean cruise on the *Fascination* are

   _____

5. A place of interest at the port of Ocho Rios is _____.

6. Can clients get a special diet on board Carnival's ships? _____ If yes, explain how you arrange it?

7. If clients cancel a 7 day cruise within 14 days of sailing, what charges will be made? _____

8. Carnival cruise ships are called the "Fun Ships." True or False. _____

Continue this type of research/practice using other brochures.

You will normally see the crew working around the clock to keep the ship in shape. After returning to port, it may only be a few hours before the next group of passengers comes aboard. The amount of supplies needed to accommodate cruise passengers is phenomenal; the weekly grocery bill alone could exceed $100,000. Some sample shopping list items for the Norway include: 65,900 eggs, 550 gallons of ice cream, 14,700 pounds of potatoes, 3,000 pounds of tomatoes, 3,000 pounds of onions, 2,000 pounds of lobster, 1,800 pounds of shrimp, and 1,200 pounds of coffee!

Using the Deck Plans of Ships

It is very important for agents to study and interpret the deck plans of ships with great care. Some of the problems and confusing areas are listed below.

CABIN SIZE—Deck plans may be misleading when showing cabins. There may be a wide variation in the size and configuration within a cabin category. Check with the cruise line reservationist for details on the cabin that may not be evident on the deck plan.

BED TYPES—Be sure to note symbols on the legend of the deck plan that may denote twin beds, queen size beds, and so on. Be sure to ask the clients' preference and confirm the type of beds with the cruise line reservationist.

NOISE—Cabins located near elevators, galleys, discos, or lounges will be subject to more noise. Cabins located under promenade or jogging decks may also have a noise problem.

PORTHOLES VERSUS WINDOWS—If the description of the outside stateroom says "window," then there is a window. If nothing is mentioned, the outside cabin most likely has a porthole (which may be sealed).

OBSTRUCTED VIEWS—Staterooms on the promenade decks will often feature views in their description. Windows may look out on a promenade deck and are not mirrored—which means the cabin is on display to all those who walk by. In addition, many times cabins or suites on these decks have views obstructed by lifeboats. Look carefully at the photos of the ship and request detailed information from the cruise line.

The Cruise Products

There is definitely something for everyone in the cruise marketplace because so many ships and destinations have entered the picture.

There are large ships, small ships, and mid-size ships. There are short cruises, medium-length cruises, and long cruises. There are cruises that cater to sophisticated travelers, casual travelers, groups, families, and special interest travelers.

The Caribbean is where nearly 60% of cruisers end up, with typical cruises stopping at four or five ports in seven days. Some have stops at private islands for an exclusive beach party atmosphere.

But for those who want to really travel, there are cruises in the Baltic Sea, the Mediterranean, the Greek Islands, Indonesia, China, and more. The sailings may be seasonal, but the excitement can be felt year-round for cruises to exotic or European destinations.

Agents should try and experience for themselves a variety of ships. They should attend conferences, seminars, and cruise line presentations. *Travel Trade* magazine offers a number of "Cruise-A-Thons" every year, so agents can complete ship inspections and gain valuable knowledge and experience. Agents who wish to specialize in cruises should put together a whole library and reference/resource center of their own. Agents can build a binder of information that includes reference brochures, sample menus, shore excursion offers, and so on. Articles from magazines and newspapers can be added to this resource guide.

Agents can learn from experiences of clients, so follow-ups are important. Agents may even want to ask particular clients to complete a cruise ship evaluation form that will aid in the agent/agency's knowledge of a new ship or one not really familiar to the staff. Making a cruise chart is another useful sales tool (described later in this chapter).

Agents should note that once a year most cruise ships go into dry-dock for two weeks for repairs and maintenance. It is helpful to know when the ship is scheduled for dry-dock and when the ship was last refurbished.

Knowledge of cruise lines and ships along with effective qualifying skills are the two main ingredients in selling cruises professionally.

What Happened to "Free Air"

Cruise lines offered air/sea packages because they were able to build the flight costs into the cruise fare. Marketing conditions have drastically reduced the amount of airline seats available to cruise lines. Often in an air/sea package the airline tickets are issued at the last minute. Passengers can sometimes get better airfares separate from the cruise and the flight schedules might be much better. In addition, sometimes the flight itineraries arranged by the cruise lines are not eligible for frequent flyer mileage. The inconveniences when you book your air separately can be in arranging the transportation to and from the airport and handling your luggage, although some cruise lines offer airport transfers. Princess Cruises' Flight Choice program gives passengers their flight information 60 days prior. The line's two air programs are Seabird Air (which automatically assigns flights to cruises) and Seaboard Gold, which allows customers to choose alternate dates, first or business class seating, or a preferred airline. Air adjustments begin at $35.00 per person plus any additional costs associated with flights.

Ship Profiles

As mentioned previously, agents may decide to create a file on ships. Here are a few profiles of ships:

SHIP: *Fantasy*
CRUISE LINE: Carnival Cruises
Registry: Liberia
Tonnage: 70,367
Officers and Crew: Italian & Int'l
Staff No.: 920
Passenger Capacity: 2,600
No. of Cabins: 1,022
Built: 1989
Refurbished: –
Former Name(s):
Facilities: Spa, health club, infirmary, casino, two dining rooms, 11 bars and lounges, skeet shooting, barbershop, beauty shop, three swimming pools, tour office, duty free shops, jogging track, four elevators, six whirlpools.

SHIP: *Costa Classica*
CRUISE LINE: Costa Cruise Line
Registry: Italy
Tonnage: 53,700
Officers and Crew: Italian & Int'l
Staff No.: 750
Passenger Capacity: 1,300
No. of Cabins: 534
Built: 1992
Refurbished: –
Former Name(s):
Facilities: Spa/gymnasium, infirmary, casino, Tivoli restaurant, La Trattoria outdoor garden with buffets, cafés, bars and lounges, showroom, disco, children's services, beauty shop, outdoor pools, whirlpools, shops, library, chapel, laundry, tour office.

SHIP: *Norway*
CRUISE LINE: Norwegian Cruise Line
Registry: Bahamas
Tonnage: 75,000
Officers and Crew: Norwegian and Int'l
Staff No.: 900
Passenger Capacity: 2,044
No. of Cabins: 904
Built: 1960
Refurbished: 1979, 1987, 1990
Former Name(s): S/S France
Facilities: Children's program and playroom, 11 passenger decks, color TV, health and fitness center, casino, two dining rooms, several bars and lounges, three pools, duty-free shops, sauna, massage, racquetball.

SHIP: *Majesty of the Seas*
CRUISE LINE: Royal Caribbean Cruise Line
Registry: Norway
Tonnage: 75,000
Officers and Crew: International
Staff No.: 827
Passenger Capacity: 2,354
No. of Cabins: 1,177
Built: 1992
Refurbished: –
Former Name(s):
Facilities: French, Italian, Caribbean, and Continental cuisine, live music in the Paint Your Wagon and Blue Skies lounges, Schooner Piano Bar, casino, gym and jogging track, shuffleboard, two outdoor pools, two whirlpools, tour office, shops, library, meeting room to seat 100, babysitting, game room, laundry.

SHIP: *Crown Dynasty*
CRUISE LINE: Crown Cruise Line
Registry: Panama
Tonnage: 20,000
Officers and Crew: Scandinavian and Filipino
Staff No.: 320
Passenger Capacity: 800
No. of Cabins: 400
Built: 1993
Refurbished: –
Former Name(s):
Facilities: Bon Vivant Dining Room features tiered seating, windows on three sides, and a skylight, Broadway-style shows and dancing in the Rhapsody Lounge, library, pool bar, casino with poker, roulette, blackjack and slots, outdoor pool, three whirlpools, fitness spa, shops, teen center, medical facilities.

SHIP: *Statendam*
CRUISE LINE: Holland America
Registry: Bahamas
Tonnage: 50,000
Officers and Crew: Dutch and Indonesian/Filipino
Staff No.: 571
Passenger Capacity: 1,264
No. of Cabins: 633
Built: 1992
Refurbished: –
Former Name(s):
Facilities: Two-deck Rotterdam Dining Room with three-sided view and dramatic grand staircase entry, several bars and lounges, Van Gogh show lounge with live entertainment, movie theater, health spa, two outdoor pools, whirlpools, card room, jogging track, shops, meeting rooms, laundry, and medical facilities.

CHAPTER 5, TEST 5

Using the information provided on the various ships, answer the questions below:

1. The tonnage of the *Majesty of the Seas* is _____.
2. Nationalities of the officers and crew on the *Statendam* are_____,
_____, and _____.
3. The _____ was built in 1993.
4. Which ship has a "Paint Your Wagon" lounge? _____
5. S/S_____ is the former name of the *Norway*.
6. The Kyoto Restaurant on the *Crystal Harmony* seats _____.
7. Both the _____ and the _____ have Italian officers.
8. All of the ships have whirlpools. True or False _____
9. The _____ has the most cabins.
10. The _____ has the least amount of cabins.

For each of the ships give:

	TONNAGE	PASSENGER CAPACITY
11. *Fantasy*	_____	_____
12. *Costa Classica*	_____	_____
13. *Norway*	_____	_____
14. *Crystal Harmony*	_____	_____
15. *Statendam*	_____	_____

Identify the ship by the number of crew to passenger capacity given:

16. 750 to 1,300 _____
17. 827 to 2,354 _____
18. 320 to 800 _____
19. 920 to 2,600 _____
20. 545 to 960 _____

Sample Reference Information

The *Official Cruise Guide* provides thorough details on ships and itineraries, booking procedures, worldwide cruising areas, and ports of call. Below is a sample ship profile of the *Crystal Harmony:*

MS CRYSTAL HARMONY

Built: 1990 Refurbished: 1997
Country of Registry: Bahamas
Classification: World Class

Ship to Shore Phone Number: 110-3237
Ship to Shore Fax Number: 110-3234

Crystal Cruises, 2121 Avenue of the Stars, Ste. 200, Los Angeles, CA 90067. (800) 446-6645

SHIP SPECIFICATIONS	LENGTH in ft.	BEAM in ft.	SPEED in knots	STABILIZED
	791	97	22	YES

GRT in cu. ft.	OFFICER'S NATIONALITY	CREW'S NATIONALITY
49,000	Norwegian/Japanese	International

LANGUAGES SPOKEN BY CREW	SIZE OF CREW	ELEVATORS
- - - - -	545	9

PASSENGER DECKS	TOTAL CABINS	SPACE RATIO PER PASSENGER IN CU.FT.
8	480	52

REGULAR PASSENGER CAPACITY	TOTAL PASSENGER CAPACITY
960	960

FACILITIES FOR THE HANDICAPPED:

4 outside cabins with wheelchair and ramp access, wide bathroom doors

CLIENTELE PROFILE: Singles 15% Couples (35-55) 15% Couples (over 55) 65% Families 5%

NATIONALITY: American 85% OTHER: 15%

TIPPING GUIDELINES:

Cabin Steward	$3.50 pp per day	Deck Steward	15% of the bill
Waiter	$3.50 pp per day	Maître d'	Individual discretion
Busboy	$2.00 pp per day	Wine Steward	15% of the bill

continued

TYPES OF PAYMENT ACCEPTED ON BOARD:

Cash, MasterCard, Visa, Travelers Checks.
Personal checks accepted and there is an on board charge system.

DESCRIPTION:

An elegantly appointed cruise ship that offers advanced technology and extremely high standards of personal service. One of the highlights of its design is a two-story atrium lobby featuring hand-cut glass sculptures and a waterfall.

ACCOMMODATIONS: Large staterooms with air conditioning, sitting area, closet, combination tub/shower, hair dryer, bathrobe, nine-channel TV (with a 24-hour news channel and sports), VCR, five-channel radio, phone, personal safe, 110AC/220AC power. Most staterooms have private verandahs. Penthouse suites with dining area, wet bar, living room, king size bed, marble accented baths with circular Jacuzzi tub and 24-hour butler service. Staterooms available for non-smokers. 24-hour room service. Personalized wake-up calls.

(The *Official Cruise Guide* also provides an outline and chart of the types of cabins with their size in square feet.)

DINING/ENTERTAINMENT:

Crystal Dining Room (International Cuisine)   Seats 500
Kyoto Restaurant (Japanese Cuisine)   Seats 60
Prego (Italian Cuisine)   Seats 55
Number of seatings for dinner: 2—hours 6:30 pm and 8:30 pm

Fine dining is available in the Crystal Dining Room or two alternative dining rooms. Indoor/outdoor Lido Cafe and The Grill. Special diets catered. Crystal Cove with crystal piano. The Bistro (a wine and coffee bar). Galaxy Show Lounge. Movies. Avenue Saloon with nightly entertainment. Club 2100 cabaret nightclub. Vista Observation Lounge featuring a harpist. Palm Court Lounge. Stars Disco. Casino in the shape of a Roman Forum.

FACILITIES AND SERVICES:

Crystal Spa and Salon with ocean view, featuring aerobics, exercise classes and equipment, saunas, steam rooms, trainers, and massage. Large lap pool with two Jacuzzis. Indoor/outdoor pool with swim-up bar and sliding glass roof. Deck sports. Jogging deck. Priests and rabbis on high holidays. Business services. Hairdresser. Shops. Tour office. Laundry and dry cleaning services. Medical facilities.

SAILING SCHEDULE: Six- to 19-day cruises to Mexican Riviera, Hawaii, Alaska/Canada, Orient, Australia/New Zealand, and the South Pacific.

The *Official Cruise Guide* also provides a deck plan of the ship, detailed itineraries, and booking information.

A variety of references should be on hand for the agent to use in the selection process. The *Berlitz Complete Guide to Cruising* provides evaluative results, ratings, and comments. Although the comments are strictly personal, they help guide agents and clients in formulating their own opinions. Technical and specific information on each ship is given, followed by a point-by-point evaluation of the various aspects of the ship. The overall positive and negative points of each ship are summarized in the comments. A sample of the information provided regarding the *Crystal Harmony*.

MV CRYSTAL HARMONY

    PRINCIPAL CRUISING AREAS: Worldwide

Cruise Line/Operator: Crystal Cruise
Former Names: None
Gross Registered Tonnage: 49,000
Built: Mitsubishi Heavy Industries (Japan)
First Entered Service: July 24, 1990
Last Refurbished: ---
Country of Registry: Bahamas
Radio Call Sign: C6IP2 Satellite Phone Number: 1103237 Fax: 1103242
Length (feet/meters): 790.5/240.96 Beam (feet/meters): 97.1/29.60
Draft (feet/meters): 24.6/7.50 Machinery: Twin-screw Mitsubishi diesel
Passenger Decks: 8 Number of Crew: 545
Passenger Capacity (basis 2): 960
Passenger Space Ratio (basis 2): 52
Officers: Norwegian/Japanese Service Staff: International
Total Cabins: 480
Size Range: 183–948 sq. ft. Door Width: 24–29″
Outside Cabins: 461 Inside Cabins: 19 Single Cabins: 0
Wheelchair-Accessible Cabins: 4
Electric Current in Cabins: 110/220 AC
Dining Rooms: 3 Sittings: 2 (dinner only, main restaurant)
Elevators: 9 Door Width: 33–35″
Casino: Yes Slot Machines: Yes
Swimming Pools (outdoor): 2 (1 is indoor/outdoor)
Whirlpools: 2 Gymnasium: Yes Sauna: Yes Massage: Yes
Cinema/Theater: Yes Number of Seats: 270
Cabin TV: Yes VCR: Yes Library: Yes
Children's Facilities/Playroom: Yes

continued

RATINGS:

Ship Appearance/Condition	93	Cleanliness	95
Passenger Space	93	Passenger Comfort Level	94
Furnishings/Decor	94	Cuisine	92
Food Service	92	Beverage Service	92
Accommodations	92	Cabin Service	92
Itineraries/Destinations	91	Shore Excursion Program	92
Entertainment	91	Activities Program	86
Cruise Director/Staff	86	Officers/Purser's Staff	87
Fitness/Sports Facilities	90	Overall Ship Facilities	92
Value for Money	90	Total Cruise Experience	90

OVERALL RATING: 1824   AVERAGE: 91.2

COMMENTS: A graceful and handsome ship in a contemporary style. Excellent open deck and sun-bathing space as well as sports facilities. Two outdoor pools (one with a swim-up bar). Several business centers that feature laptop computers. Outstanding public lounges, which include the Vista-Observation Lounge and the restful, elegant Palm Court Lounge. Excellent in-cabin television. Elegant dining rooms and excellent silver service. Spacious, well-designed staterooms—including four spectacular Crystal penthouses. More than half the staterooms have private verandahs, but the bathrooms are somewhat compact. Ample drawer space, but closet hanging space may be limited for long voyages. It is a most outstanding ship.

CHAPTER 5, TEST 6

Using the sample information given for the *Crystal Harmony* answer these questions:

1. How many cabins are there?_____

2. What is the passenger capacity?_____

3. When was the ship built?_____

4. When was it last refurbished? _____

5. What is the nationality of the crew?_____

6. What percentage of cruise passengers do families represent?_____

7. American passengers comprise approximately _____% of the total passengers.

8. How many single cabins are there?_____

9. What is the passenger to space ratio?_____

10. What are the nationalities of the officers?_____

11. How many crew members are there?_____

12. There are _____ elevators.

13. How many wheelchair-accessible cabins are there?_____

14. The ship has a length of _____ and a beam of _____.

15. Its tonnage is _____.

16. There are _____ inside cabins and _____ outside cabins.

17. The main dining room is called the _____.

18. The ship was built by _____ Industries.

19. According to the Berlitz guide, it rates an overall 1824 and an average of _____.

20. The Prego dining room seats _____ passengers.

21. The Kyoto dining room seats _____.

22. The cabaret night club is called _____.

23. Most staterooms have private verandahs. True or False_____

24. The ship-to-shore phone number is _____.

25. The ship's speed in knots is _____.

A Sample Agent–Client Conversation

The following is a sample conversation between an agent and a client. The departure is several months away.

AGENT: Hello, my name is Barbara. How may I help you?

CLIENTS: We are interested in taking a cruise.

AGENT: Wonderful! Have you been on cruises before?

CLIENTS: Yes. Last year we sailed on the *Oceanic* to the Bahamas. This time we would like to try a seven-day cruise.

AGENT: Fine. Let's get started with your name, address, and phone number, please.

CLIENTS: Mr. and Mrs. Gimpyl, 14330 N. 15th St., Oklahoma City, OK 77744. Our phone number is (555) 444-3333.

AGENT: Are you both U.S. citizens and do you have proof of citizenship, preferably a passport?

CLIENTS: We both have valid U.S. passports.

AGENT: Good. Since you have stated your interest in a seven-day cruise, most of the Caribbean cruises leave on Saturday or Sunday from the ports of Miami or Ft. Lauderdale. What dates did you have in mind, and do you have a preference for a departure point?

CLIENTS: We are planning this for sometime in April, and we don't really have a preference for the departure port.

AGENT: There would be several ships to choose from for either Miami or Ft. Lauderdale. Are there particular ports you would like to visit?

CLIENTS: Oh, we would like to see St. Thomas, and we have heard that the island of St. Maarten is nice.

AGENT: Let me get a few brochures for cruise ships that visit those destinations and we can go over some details about the type of services and specifics of the ships.

As mentioned before, cruise ship evaluations can be done at various conferences and on "fam trips." In addition, agents may want to ask valued clients for their opinions and evaluation of ships when appropriate. A sample cruise ship evaluation form can be found below.

CRUISE SHIP EVALUATION

DATE: _____   COMPLETED BY: _____

LENGTH OF CRUISES _____   RANGE OF RATES _____

CABINS/STATEROOMS   # _____   # _____   # _____   # _____

SIZE OF ROOM (S,M,L or sq.ft)   _____   _____   _____   _____

BERTHS (U&L=upper/lower   2L=2 lowers, Q=queen bed, etc.)

_____   _____   _____   _____

FLOOR COVERING (carpet/other)   _____   _____   _____   _____

DECOR (rate 1–5 with 5 for best)   _____   _____   _____   _____

DRAWER SPACE (L-lots/N-not much) ____ CLOSET SPACE–GENERALLY (L-lots, N-not much) ____

BATHROOM–COMMENTS: _____

STANDARD CABIN AMENITIES: ____ TV ____ RADIO ____ REFRIGERATOR ____ NIGHT LIGHT

____ BOTTLE OPENER ____ DRINKABLE WATER ____ CLOTHESLINE ____ HANGERS

____ 110 V. OUTLET FOR HAIR DRYER ____ RAZOR OUTLET ____ LARGE MIRROR

____ WRITING SHELF/DESK OTHER _____

SUPERIOR CABIN AMENITIES: ____ TV ____ RADIO ____ REFRIGERATOR ____ NIGHT LIGHT

____ BOTTLE OPENER ____ DRINKABLE WATER ____ CLOTHESLINE ____ HANGERS

____ 110 V. OUTLET FOR HAIR DRYER ____ RAZOR OUTLET ____ LARGE MIRROR

____ WRITING SHELF/DESK OTHER _____

RATE THE FOLLOWING WITH A SCORE OF 1 TO 5 (5 IS BEST) AND TOTAL EACH AREA:

LOUNGES AND PUBLIC AREAS

Decor _____ Cleanliness _____ Lighting _____ Roominess _____ Seating Comfort _____

Temperature _____ Ventilation _____ Noise Level _____ Acoustics _____ Dance Areas _____

Bar Accessibility _____ Waiter Services _____ Views _____

TOTAL _____

DECK AREAS AND POOL(S)

Deck size _____ Pool Size _____ Shaded Areas _____ Deck Chairs Comfort _____

Deck Chairs Availability _____ Deck Surface _____ Pool Features _____ Cleanliness _____

Safety Features _____ Towel Service _____ Waiter Services _____ Acceptable Noise Level _____

Entertainment/Games (if applicable) _____

TOTAL _____

DINING AREAS

Decor _____ Cleanliness _____ Lighting _____ Roominess _____ Seating Comfort _____

Temperature _____ Ventilation _____ Acceptable Noise Level _____

TOTAL _____

OF TABLES FOR   TWO _____ FOUR _____ SIX _____ EIGHT _____ TWELVE _____

DINING SERVICE

Promptness _____ Efficiency _____ Courtesy _____ Professionalism _____   TOTAL _____

FOOD AND BEVERAGES

Quality _____ Quantity _____ Variety _____ Appropriate Temperature _____ Presentation _____

Wine Selection _____ Drinks Selection _____ Reasonable Cost For Beverages _____

Special Diets Available _____

TOTAL _____

ENTERTAINMENT

Quality _____ Variety _____ Professionalism _____   TOTAL _____

PASSAGEWAYS

Width _____ Height _____ Lighting _____ Floor Surface _____ Hand Rails _____

Ashtrays _____ Freedom from obstructions _____ Suitable for Special Needs _____

TOTAL _____

CABIN SERVICE

Promptness _____ Courtesy _____ Efficiency _____ Professionalism _____   TOTAL _____

CABIN FOOD SERVICE (Indicate N/A if not applicable)

Prompt _____ Presentation _____ Appropriate Temperature _____ Quality _____ Quantity _____

Other comments _____   TOTAL _____

continued

THEATRE

Accessible _____ Seating Comfort _____ Roomingness _____ View _____ Acoustics _____ Lighting _____

Temperature _____ Movie Selection _____ Program Frequency _____   TOTAL _____

OTHER FACILITIES (Indicate N/A if not applicable)

SHOPS _____ PURSER'S OFFICE _____ TOUR DESK _____ CHAPEL _____ HOSPITAL _____

SAUNA _____ ELEVATOR OPERATIONS _____/AVAILABILITY _____ EXERCISE ROOM _____

INDOOR POOL _____ CHILDREN'S PLAYROOM _____ STAIRWAYS _____

PHOTO SHOP _____ BEAUTY SALON _____ CASINO _____ SLOT MACHINES _____

FULL CASINO _____ CASINO SERVICES _____   TOTAL _____

OTHER SERVICES

DANCE/AEROBIC CLASSES _____ CRAFT CLASSES _____ ORGANIZED GAMES _____

LECTURES _____ CRUISE DIRECTOR _____ EASE OF EMBARKATION _____/DEBARKATION _____

INFORMATION _____ CHILDREN'S ACTIVITIES _____

EXCURSIONS/TOURS AT PORTS _____ BULLETINS _____   TOTAL _____

GRAND TOTAL = _____

TIPPING POLICIES AND PROCEDURES: _____

_____

_____

BASIC CLASSIFICATION OF SHIP: _____ DELUXE   _____ FIRST CLASS   _____ STANDARD

SHIP IS MOST LIKELY TO DRAW (check all that apply):   _____ couples   _____ families

_____ honeymooners   _____ business clients   _____ singles   _____ tourists   _____ students

_____ elderly   _____ first time cruisers   _____ experienced cruisers   _____ adventure seekers

BUSIEST MONTHS FOR THIS SHIP WOULD BE _____

SPECIAL RATES: _____

TRANSPORTATION TO PORT/PIER DETAILS _____

_____

_____

PIER FACILITIES AND SERVICES (rate 1 to 5 with 5 being the best):

Cleanliness _____ Air Temperature _____ Baggage Handling _____ Lighting _____ Staff Efficiency _____

Parking Facilities _____ Roominess _____ Seating Comfort _____ Customs Inspection Facilities _____

Weather Protected _____

OTHER DETAILS/SPECIFICS/COSTS _____

_____

OTHER COMMENTS: _____

_____

Making a Cruise Chart

A useful tool for selling cruises is a cruise chart. You can develop this chart showing cruises from an area based on their length. Use current issues of reference books and magazines for compiling the data and make an effort to keep it updated. You will learn about ships, lines, itineraries, ports of embarkation, and other details by making a chart.

Sample Cruise Chart for Cruises from Florida:

This is for example only and may not reflect current data.

LENGTH	LEAVES FROM	TO	SHIP	LINE
1@	Pt. Manatee	nowhere	Regal Empress	Regal
1	Ft. Lauderdale	Freeport	Discovery	Discovery Sun
3&4 3-Thu. 4-Sun.	Pt.Canaveral	Nassau* * & FPO	Fantasy	Carnival
3&4 3-Fri. 4-Mon.	Miami	Nassau* * & FPO	Ecstasy	Carnival
4-Mon.	Miami	EYW, CZM	Norwegian Majesty	NCL
3&4 3-Fri. 4-Mon.	Miami	Nassau+ EYW,+Great Stirrup Cay, NAS	Norwegian Sea	NCL
3&4 3-Fri. 4-Mon.	Miami	NAS, Coco Cay NAS, Coco Cay, EYW	Majesty of the Seas	RCI
4-Alt.Thu. 5-Alt.Mon and Sat.	Tampa	EYW, CUN, CZM GCM, CUN, CZM	Jubilee	Carnival
7-Alt. Sat.	Miami	CUN, CZM, GCM, Ocho Rios	Carnival Triumph	Carnival
7-Alt.Sat		SJU, STT, STX		
7-Alt.Sun.	Miami	SJU, STX, STT	Carnival Victory	Carnival
7-Alt.Sun.		CUN, CZM, GCM, Ocho Rios		

@certain dates, then the ship does 3,4,5,7,10,11 and other length cruises

There are several more seven-night cruises to list from Miami as well as Ft. Lauderdale.

Note: City/codes and other abbreviations have been used, such as FPO for Freeport, NCL for Norwegian Cruise Line, RCL for Royal Caribbean International, EYW for Key West, CZM for Cozumel, and CUN for Cancun (port is Playa del Carmen). Also Ft. Lauderdale is shown, but ships leave from Port Everglades.

You can add other columns to show the number of tonnage, passengers, crew, crew nationality, prices, and special details (discounts, promotions, etc.).

CHAPTER 5, REVIEW 1

1. What are the possible advantages and disadvantages of booking flights separately from the air/sea program that might be offered by the cruise line?

   _____

   _____

   _____

2. What are the advantages of agents working with a select group of cruise lines and ships?

   _____

   _____

   _____

3. How can agents handle the situation when they are faced with advertised discounted prices that aren't available to the agency?

   _____

   _____

   _____

   _____

   _____

4. What factors can influence the cost of a cruise?

   _____

   _____

5. There may be obstructed views on the promenade decks. What should an agent do about giving information on the view from a client's stateroom/cabin? _____

   _____

   _____

6. Why are the previous cruise experiences of the client important? _____

   _____

   _____

7. What is a repositioning cruise? _____

   _____

   _____

8. Why are guarantees usually good deals? _____

   _____

9. What area of the world handles about 60% of cruisers?

_____

10. What do you think are the advantages of using videos as part of the sales process?

_____

_____

_____

11. What are possible disadvantages of using videos?

_____

_____

_____

12. A sample formula for gifts for clients can be $_____ for every $_____ spent.

13. When and why should agents recommend travel insurance? _____

_____

_____

14. Name four items of information that the agent should check when examining the cruise tickets/documents.

_____

_____

15. Why should agents use open-ended questions when dealing with clients?

_____

_____

Optional Exercise: Research Activities

In order to be a cruise specialist, you must be familiar with cruise lines, ships, itineraries, destinations, specifics, and other details. Using references such as the *Official Steamship Guide, Official Cruise Guide,* cruise brochures, or other resources, answer these questions. Some sections may be completed using information provided in this manual.

1. How many tons is the *Queen Elizabeth 2?* _____.

2. Name two cities from which a Rhine cruise can be taken. _____

3. From what pier at Miami does the *Norway* sail? _____

4. Is there port-to-port service from Haines, Alaska, to Prince Rupert, British Columbia, Canada? _____

5. Name two stops usually included on Nile cruises leaving from Aswan. _____

6. Three ships that have three- and four-night cruises to the Bahamas from Miami are _____

_____

7. How many passengers does the *Holiday* normally carry? _____

8. In what country is the *Fascination* registered? _____

9. Is there a hydrofoil service between Sorrento and Naples, Italy? _____

10. Name two freighter companies that accept passengers. _____

_____

Name two ships operated by each of the following cruise lines.

Note: This section can be completed using the list provided in this manual.

11. CARNIVAL _____

12. NORWEGIAN CRUISE LINE _____

13. CUNARD _____

14. PRINCESS _____

15. ROYAL CARIBBEAN _____

16. HOLLAND AMERICA _____

17. COSTA _____

18. CELEBRITY _____

19. DELTA QUEEN STEAMBOAT COMPANY _____

20. CRYSTAL CRUISES _____

Using an atlas if necessary, match the ports to the islands/cities/countries applicable: Some answers may be used more than once.

21. _____ San Juan

22. _____ Ocho Rios

23. _____ La Guaira

24. _____ Charlotte Amalie

25. _____ Nassau

26. _____ Playa del Carmen

27. _____ Piraeus

28. _____ Willemstad

29. _____ Oranjestad

30. _____ Freeport

31. _____ Philipsburg

32. _____ Montego Bay

33. _____ Georgetown

A. Athens, Greece

B. Aruba

C. Grand Cayman, Cayman Is.

D. St. Thomas, U.S.V.I.

E. Jamaica

F. Curacao

G. New Providence Is., Bahamas

H. Puerto Rico

I. St. Maarten

J. Grand Bahama Is., Bahamas

K. Cancun, Mexico

L. Caracas, Venezuela

CHAPTER 6

Reservations, Payments, and Tickets

HIGHLIGHTS OF THIS CHAPTER INCLUDE:

- ✦ Making Reservations
- ✦ Payments
- ✦ Tickets
- ✦ Other Forms Agencies May Use
- ✦ Travel Checklists, Useful Forms, and Pamphlets
- ✦ Sample Role-Play Activities

MAKING RESERVATIONS

If booking a cruise through a computer reservation system, follow the instructions and formats required. If booking on-line, follow the prompts or instructions. When phoning for a reservation, here are some important specifics.

First, always have the brochure in hand when making reservations.

From the Client

1. Obtain the information and fill out a reservation form, if possible. Select cruise line, ship, date(s).

2. Make certain to ask the citizenship of the clients, since documentary requirements vary.

3. Ask what category/type of cabin they might prefer. Don't just select a cabin. After checking with the cruise line, explain what is available. If the cruise line offers a choice of cabins, show the clients the deck plan and point out the cabins available. Circle the cabin that has been selected.

4. Obtain meal sitting preference and any other requests.

From the Cruise Line

1. Confirm cabin number (unless it is to be assigned [TBA]).

2. Reconfirm prices per person, port taxes, air/sea add-ons, if applicable, any other fees, and the total due.

3. If clients will be paying by credit card, find out payment processing procedures, unless you are already familiar with the process.

4. If it is an air/sea program, confirm any details. If the flight information is available, write the schedule down so that you can give an itinerary to the clients.

5. Obtain deposit option date and final payment deadline (or total payment deadline if a short-notice booking).

6. Get the name of the person and a confirmation/reservation number, and write this down with the date of confirmation.

AFTER RESERVATIONS HAVE BEEN CONFIRMED:

On the client's copy of the brochure, circle the cabin selected, and underline or highlight the prices, itinerary, cancellation penalties, and other important specifics. If available, give the clients the flight schedules. Write down payment deadlines for them. Answer any questions.

The cruise reservation/inquiry form (a sample is provided) can help you make reservations efficiently.

CRUISE RESERVATION/INQUIRY FORM

NAME(S): _____ CITIZENSHIP _____

ADDRESS _____

PHONE(S) home _____ work _____ E-mail_____

NO.OF

ADULTS _____ CHILDREN _____ AGES _____ PREVIOUS CRUISES:_____

_____

DEPARTURE   NO.OF

DATE(S)_____ALTERNATIVES_____DAYS_____

- -

1st CRUISE LINE: _____ SHIP _____

PHONE # _____ SAILING DATE _____

CABIN CATEGORY/TYPE REQUESTED _____

CATEGORY/CABIN CONFIRMED: _____ DECK _____

MEAL SITTING _____ OTHER SPECIFICS _____

_____

CONFIRMATION # _____ BY _____ DATE _____

PRICES _____ per person _____ air/sea _____ cruise only

Port taxes _____ other charges _____

TOTAL DUE _____ DEPOSIT _____ OPTION DATE _____

FINAL PAYMENT _____ DUE _____

Payment made by ___ cash ___ check ___ credit card: _____

Payment made by ___ cash ___ check ___ credit card: _____

- -

2ND CRUISE LINE: _____ SHIP _____

PHONE # _____ SAILING DATE _____

CABIN CATEGORY/TYPE REQUESTED _____

CATEGORY/CABIN CONFIRMED: _____ DECK _____

MEAL SITTING _____ OTHER SPECIFICS _____

_____

CONFIRMATION # _____ BY _____ DATE _____

PRICES _____ per person _____ air/sea _____ cruise only

Port taxes _____ other charges _____

TOTAL DUE _____ DEPOSIT _____ OPTION DATE _____

FINAL PAYMENT _____ DUE _____

Payment made by ___ cash ___ check ___ credit card: _____

Payment made by ___ cash ___ check ___ credit card: _____

- -

AIR/SEA PACKAGE INCLUDES: _____

FLIGHTS: _____

TICKETS RECEIVED/DONE _____CRUISE _____FLIGHTS   GIVEN TO CLIENT ON_____ DATE

OTHER: ___Bon Voyage Gift:_____

___Travel Bag/Passport wallet ___Travel Checklist, Cruise Information Sheet

___Insurance Waiver/Information Other _____

FOLLOW UP_____ DATE _____

A/S—Air/Sea

BTH—Bath

CFMD BY—Confirmed by

DBL—Double

DEP—Deposit

DOCS RECD—Documents received

EB—Eastbound

F/P—Final payment

GTD or GUAR—Guaranteed

I/S—Inside cabin

M/M—Mr. and Mrs.

OPT—Option

O/S—Outside cabin

OW—One way

PP—Per person

PSGR ADVSD—Passenger advised

PT—Port taxes

QUAD—Four people accommodated

RT—Round trip

SGL—Single

TBA—To be assigned

TPL—Triple

WB—Westbound

WL—Waitlist

Abbreviations for beds: D = Double, Q = Queen, 2S = 2 Singles, U & L—Upper and Lower

These are just samples. Check the brochure specifics for other codes that may be used.

Cruise Booking Terms

Add on—A supplementary amount.

Air/Sea—A package combining the air fare and cruise rate.

Booking—A reservation.

Cruise Only—The rate for the cruise, not including air fare.

Fly/Cruise—*See* air/sea.

Gratuities—Tips.

Guarantee—Agreement to provide expected services or products. A rate that is protected against increases. A special fare extended because the cabin will be assigned at the time of sailing.

Guarantee Share Rate—A special fare extended to a single passenger who agrees to the assignment of a cabin mate by the cruise line. The line will ask age, gender, and if a smoker/non-smoker and attempt a match with another passenger.

Open sitting—No table assignments made.

Option date—Date by which payment must be received or the reservations will be cancelled.

Run of the Ship Rate—Low fare offered because cabin is assigned by the cruise line. Also called a guarantee rate.

Shore excursions—Tours at ports which usually cost extra.

Stand By—Waiting list for passengers on a sold-out cruise.

Upper & Lower—Like bunk beds.

Waitlist—List established for those passengers waiting for possible cancellations.

Example of a Call for Cruise Reservations

Note: Always have the brochure handy when calling for reservations.

A = CRUISE RESERVATIONS AGENT

B = TRAVEL AGENT

A: West Indies Cruises Reservations. May I help you?

B: Yes, please. This is Irma from Adventure Travel in Atlanta. I am checking for reservations on the *Atlantic Odyssey,* departing July 15, requesting cabin category H or the least expensive available.

A: Let me check availability. We can give you a guarantee for category H—cabin number to be assigned. Can I have the last name of the passengers?

B: Yes, the party is Mr. John Hunter and Mrs. Elizabeth Hunter. They would like first sitting for meals.

A: Confirming Mr. and Mrs. Hunter on the *Atlantic Odyssey,* July 15, and first sitting for meals. The air/sea rate is $1,895.00 per person plus $189.00 port charges per person. A deposit of $500.00 is due one week from today; final payment is due six weeks prior.

B: Do you have any information on the flight schedules?

A: The flight schedule information will be available approximately two to three weeks prior to departure.

B: Thank you. Can I have your name and a confirmation number, please?

A: My name is Caroline, and the confirmation number is 43GR56. What is your ARC* number?

B: 12345678.

A: Thank you. Did you need any additional information or reservations?

B: No, not at this time. Thank you.

A: Thank you for calling West Indies Cruises. Have a good day!

B: Thank you. Goodbye.

The agent would go over all the details with the client, explaining the guarantee if it hasn't been explained before and providing other specifics, perhaps recommending particular shore excursions, and so on.

PAYMENTS

When clients have made a payment for a cruise (deposit or final payment), a receipt or invoice marked PAID is usually given to the client. One copy of the invoice is put on file (possibly in a folder the agent keeps at his or her desk, or in a central place), and another copy is used for accounting. A sample invoice form is shown on page 128.

*ARC = Airlines Reporting Corporation. *Note:* Another identifying number may be used when making reservations, such as a Cruise Lines International Asociation (CLIA) membership number, or other accepting organizational membership identification.

FLY AWAY TRAVEL
111 First St.
Anywhere, OH 55222
(222) 333-4444

NO. 123456

TO:

Agent	Contact	Customer #	Account #	Date

Code	Day	Date	City/Arpt.	Time	Carrier	Flt#,Class	Amount

Codes: A – AIR   H – HOTEL   C – CAR   T – TOUR   S – SURFACE
W – CRUISE   V – OTHER TRAVEL SERVICE

STATUS CODES: OK – CONFIRMED   RQ – REQUESTED   WL – WAIT LIST

Deposit Payments

When the deposit for a cruise is paid, the agency sends the amount to the cruise line. If the client pays by cash or check, the agency deposits the payment into its account and issues an agency check for the same amount.

If the client pays by credit card, contact the cruise line for processing procedures. Some cruise lines require the contractor copy of the UCCCF (Universal Credit Card Charge Form) to be mailed to them. Some will take the name, credit card number, expiration date and then process it as a phone charge.

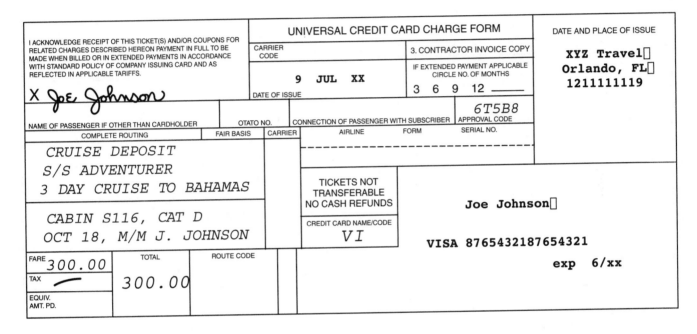

Final Payments

If the client pays the balance by cash or check, the agency deposits the amount into its account and issues an agency check for the net amount due (amount less commission). For example:

TOTAL COST = $2,400.00 (Cabin cost $2,300.00, port taxes $100.00)

DEPOSIT = $500.00 When agency receives, sends $500.00

FINAL PAYMENT = $1,900.00 Agency receives, sends net amount to cruise line. If commission is 10% (2,300 − 10%), net amount sent = $1,670.00 ($1,900 × $230).

If the client pays the balance by credit card, contact the cruise line for procedures. The line will either process it as a phone charge or require the contractor copy of the UCCCF (as explained above). After processing, the cruise line sends a commission check to the agency.

Agents should recommend/discuss insurance needs. If the client doesn't want to purchase insurance, agents may use a waiver of insurance form for the client to sign to protect the agency from circumstances that cause the clients to cancel/lose monies.

Other sample forms to use: Enclosure of brochures, correspondence with vendors, sample itinerary.

FROM: FLY AWAY TRAVEL   THANK YOU FOR YOUR INQUIRY!
            1111 First St.   We have enclosed flyers or brochures that
            Anywhere, OH 44555   pertain to your travel plans and needs.
            (222) 333-4444   Please contact us if you have any ques-
                                     tions and remember that reservations
TO: should be made as early as possible.

                                     AGENT _____

DATE: _____
FROM: FLY AWAY TRAVEL   RE CLIENTS: _____
            1111 First St.   TOUR/SHIP NAME _____
            Anywhere, OH 44555   DEPARTURE DATE: _____
            (222) 333-4444   IT# (if applicable) _____
                                     ___ Deposit of _____ enclosed
TO: ___ Final payment of _____ enclosed
                                     CHECK # _____
                                     CREDIT CARD # _____
                                     ____ Please cancel reservations
                                     ____ Refund the amount of _____

MESSAGE _____
_____
_____
_____

                                     AGENT _____

ITINERARY PREPARED FOR: _____   BY: FLY AWAY TRAVEL
                                                                    (202) 333-4444

DAY	DATE	AIRLINE, FLT.#	DEPART CITY	TIME	ARRIVE CITY	TIME	MEALS/ STOPS

TICKETS

When the final payment has been made, advise clients that tickets will usually be received two to three weeks prior to sailing. The clients can decide whether to pick up the documents or have them mailed (agents should use certified mail, return receipt requested or another traceable method). When the tickets are received, the agent should check them carefully against the reservation information to make sure everything is correct. If an air/sea program, advise the clients to reconfirm the reservation directly with the airline in case of flight schedule changes. The cruise ticket will show passenger names, ship, sailing date, cabin confirmed, possibly the meal sitting confirmed, and other information. Baggage tags are usually included. Instruct the clients to tag their luggage so that clients and baggage are directed accordingly on arrival.

It is best to go over the documents personally with the client so that all is understood and any final questions can be answered. The agency may also provide travel bags, passport wallets, brochures on the destinations, helpful information flyers, or other "goodies." Bon voyage gifts may also have been arranged. A sample cruise ticket is below.

BON VOYAGE CRUISES
43434 1st Ave. N.
Miami, FL 33333

TICKET FOR PASSAGE

TICKET # 09222435

| NAMES (NOT-TRANSFERABLE) | CABIN/STATEROOM | SHIP |
| M/M Jose Gonzalino | M 1091 | NAUTICAL WANDERER |

CATEGORY: F   No. of days: 7   Ship's Registry: Liberia

PORT OF EMBARKATION: MIAMI
PORT OF DEBARKATION: MIAMI

AGENT: Barbara
BOOKING AGENCY: Travel 4 U
12345 6th St.
Podiak, LA 55555

SAILING DATE: SEP. 25
SAILING TIME: 6:00 PM

Please read carefully the terms and conditions as outlined on the back of this passage contract.

In addition to the ticket, an immigration/documentation form is normally provided, plus helpful booklets or flyers regarding cruise specifics, port of embarkation details, and so on. A sample immgration/documention form is shown below. It is particularly helpful when agents fill these forms out for the client (or with the client's help if necessary).

NAME: _____   SEX: _____   OCCUPATION: _____

PASSPORT: _____   CITIZENSHIP: _____   STATE/PROVINCE/COUNTRY

ADDRESS: _____   OF BIRTH: _____

CITY/STATE/ZIP POSTAL CODE: _____

TELEPHONE: _____   BIRTH DATE: _____   SOC. SECURITY #: _____

In case of emergency call:

Name _____   Relationship _____   Phone(s) _____

Address _____   _____

Passenger Signature: _____   _____

OTHER FORMS AGENCIES MAY USE

FLY AWAY TRAVEL
1111 First St.
Anywhere, OH 44555
(222) 333-4444

TICKETS FOR:

Please call us for your airline, hotel, car rental, tour, cruise, reservations; vacation or business travel; group or specialty tours!

Thank you for using Fly Away Travel for your travel plans. Remember to reconfirm your reservations directly with the airline, check in at least 1½ hours prior for domestic and 2–3 hours prior for international flights. Check over your documents when you receive them. If you must change your itinerary, additional costs may be involved. Guard your ticket! Lost, stolen, or destroyed tickets cannot be refunded unless and until authority has been granted by the airline, and with an imposed service charge. Because of the possibility of an airline default or bankruptcy of a carrier or other supplier, we highly recommend the purchase of insurance. This travel agency is acting as an intermediary for the suppliers or services and is therefore not responsible for breach of contract or negligence on the part of those suppliers. This travel agency hereby gives notice that it cannot be responsible for disruption of travel, damages, or injury that results from terrorist acts, monetary crisis, political or social unrest, labor problems, mechanical or other difficulties, local laws, health or climate conditions, or outbreaks of disease.

Date: _____
RE: Invoice # _____
Invoice dated _____
Amount due _____

FROM: FLY AWAY TRAVEL
1111 First St.
Anywhere, OH 44555
(222) 333-4444

TO:

JUST A REMINDER: If the payment has already been mailed, thank you! If you have not paid the amount due, please respond immediately to this notice to hold your reservations.

TRAVEL CHECKLISTS, USEFUL FORMS, AND PAMPHLETS

In addition to the forms shown, agencies can design forms or order helpful brochures and pamphlets. Some useful items are provided by organizations such as the American Society of Travel Agents (ASTA) and Cruise Lines International Association (CLIA). Agencies designing their own materials might want to provide things like a travel checklist or a flyer about cruises. A sample travel checklist form is shown below. It can be given to clients with the documents.

TRAVEL CHECKLIST
(Use pencil so form can be reused.)

GENERAL ITEMS
____ suitcase, carry-on, garment bag
____ wallet, cash, travelers' checks
____ passport & copy, I.D., driver's license
____ visa, proof of citizenship, shots
____ airline ticket, vouchers, tickets
____ credit cards, Int'l Driving Permit
____ maps, language books, guidebooks

PERSONAL ITEMS
____ soap ____ shampoo ____ toothpaste
____ brush ____ razor ____ medicines
____ lotion ____ first aid ____ hair dryer
____ wash cloth ____ toilet paper/tissue
____ sewing kit/pins ____ birth control
OTHER _____

CLOTHING
____ slacks ____ shirts ____ ties
____ dresses/skirts ____ jackets ____ socks
____ shorts ____ underwear ____ stockings
____ walking shoes ____ dress shoes
____ swimsuit ____ sweater ____ gloves
____ sleepwear ____ slip ____ belts ____ hat
OTHER _____

USEFUL ITEMS
____ pocket knife
____ alarm clock ____ watch ____ books
____ cards ____ camera & film ____ adapter
____ insect repellent ____ binoculars
____ tennis racket/balls ____ mask/fins
____ candle/flashlight ____ clothesline ____ cards
____ laundry/souvenirs bag ____ snacks
____ water bottle ____ umbrella/raincoat
____ magazines ____ sunglasses, sunscreen
____ stationery, stamps (if appl.) ____ pen

USEFUL INFORMATION
____ stop newspaper
____ stop mail
____ pets in kennel
____ advise neighbor to watch house
____ leave key with neighbor, relative
____ turn off air conditioner
____ turn off water heater
____ unplug major appliances
____ put jewelry, valuables in safety deposit box
____ pay bills that will be due

THANK YOU FOR BOOKING WITH . . .

AGENCY NAME _____
ADDRESS _____
PHONE _____
WEBSITE _____

SAMPLE ROLE-PLAY ACTIVITIES

To prepare to handle clients, you should research details carefully. If possible, have someone be the client for the following situations. Sample cruise reservation/inquiry forms and role-play evaluation forms are provided. Use pencil when completing these forms so they can be reused. Role-play activities in a classroom setting should involve evaluation by the instructor and/or other students to evaluate communication and sales skills. Videotaping of the activities may also be helpful.

1. Mr. and Mrs. Golden Anniversary want to take a cruise on the *Norway*. They sailed on it 20 years ago when it was the *S/S France*. They would like to go the last weekend in March, and have an outside cabin on one of the upper decks.

2. Mr. and Mrs. Happy Family and their two children, Biff and Buff, want to go on an early July cruise that is combined with a stay at Disney World. They want an inexpensive rate.

3. Marilyn Manroe, Carol Chunning, and Ruby Goosebay want to go on one of Carnival Cruise Line's "Fun Ships." They don't have a ship preference and have never been on a cruise. They want to leave from Miami the last weekend in September.

4. Mr. and Mrs. Yip Yuppie want to take a cruise through the Panama Canal. They don't have any dates in mind. They need all the information.

5. Mr. Lonely Guy wants to take a cruise to the Bahamas for three or four nights, leaving the last week in April. He is a single, and wants to share a cabin if possible.

6. Mr. and Mrs. Al Adventurous are interested in cruising down the Rhine River. They already have their airline tickets—round-trip to Frankfurt, Germany. The dates of travel are June 15–July 21. They need all the details.

7. Arlene Whittlemeyer and Faye Bertrand want to buy a cruise vacation for their husbands who both have the same birthday, August 3. It is going to be a surprise, so phone calls can only be made to the ladies to discuss any details. They have $2,500 each (per couple) and want to go on a seven-day cruise from San Juan, Puerto Rico, if possible.

8. Jeanette and Barbara Cossubona want to take a cruise through the fjords of Scandinavia, leaving the last week in June.

9. Tom and Jerry Door want to go on a Greek Islands cruise sometime in August.

10. Mr. and Mrs. Caprice want to take a Mississippi River cruise in May.

CRUISE RESERVATION/INQUIRY FORM

NAME(S): _____ CITIZENSHIP _____

ADDRESS _____

PHONE(S) home _____ work _____ E-mail_____

NO.OF

ADULTS _____ CHILDREN _____ AGES _____ PREVIOUS CRUISES:_____

_____

DEPARTURE   NO.OF

DATE(S)_____ALTERNATIVES_____DAYS_____

- -

1st CRUISE LINE: _____ SHIP _____

PHONE # _____ SAILING DATE _____

CABIN CATEGORY/TYPE REQUESTED _____

CATEGORY/CABIN CONFIRMED: _____ DECK _____

MEAL SITTING _____ OTHER SPECIFICS _____

_____

CONFIRMATION # _____ BY _____ DATE _____

PRICES _____ per person ____ air/sea ____ cruise only

Port taxes _____ other charges _____

TOTAL DUE _____ DEPOSIT _____ OPTION DATE _____

FINAL PAYMENT _____ DUE _____

Payment made by ___ cash ___ check ___ credit card: _____

Payment made by ___ cash ___ check ___ credit card: _____

- -

2ND CRUISE LINE: _____ SHIP _____

PHONE # _____ SAILING DATE _____

CABIN CATEGORY/TYPE REQUESTED _____

CATEGORY/CABIN CONFIRMED: _____ DECK _____

MEAL SITTING _____ OTHER SPECIFICS _____

_____

CONFIRMATION # _____ BY _____ DATE _____

PRICES _____ per person ____ air/sea ____ cruise only

Port taxes _____ other charges _____

TOTAL DUE _____ DEPOSIT _____ OPTION DATE _____

FINAL PAYMENT _____ DUE _____

Payment made by ___ cash ___ check ___ credit card: _____

Payment made by ___ cash ___ check ___ credit card: _____

- -

AIR/SEA PACKAGE INCLUDES: _____

FLIGHTS: _____

TICKETS RECEIVED/DONE ____CRUISE ____FLIGHTS GIVEN TO CLIENT ON____ DATE

OTHER: ___Bon Voyage Gift:_____

___Travel Bag/Passport wallet ___Travel Checklist, Cruise Information Sheet

___Insurance Waiver/Information Other _____

FOLLOW UP_____ DATE _____

CRUISE RESERVATION/INQUIRY FORM

NAME(S): _____   CITIZENSHIP _____

ADDRESS _____

PHONE(S) home _____   work _____   E-mail_____

NO.OF

ADULTS _____   CHILDREN _____   AGES _____   PREVIOUS CRUISES:_____

_____

DEPARTURE   NO.OF

DATE(S)_____ALTERNATIVES_____DAYS_____

- -

1st CRUISE LINE: _____   SHIP _____

PHONE # _____   SAILING DATE _____

CABIN CATEGORY/TYPE REQUESTED _____

CATEGORY/CABIN CONFIRMED: _____   DECK _____

MEAL SITTING _____   OTHER SPECIFICS _____

_____

CONFIRMATION # _____   BY _____   DATE _____

PRICES _____ per person ____ air/sea ____ cruise only

Port taxes _____ other charges _____

TOTAL DUE _____   DEPOSIT _____   OPTION DATE _____

FINAL PAYMENT _____   DUE _____

Payment made by ___ cash ___ check ___ credit card: _____

Payment made by ___ cash ___ check ___ credit card: _____

- -

2ND CRUISE LINE: _____   SHIP _____

PHONE # _____   SAILING DATE _____

CABIN CATEGORY/TYPE REQUESTED _____

CATEGORY/CABIN CONFIRMED: _____   DECK _____

MEAL SITTING _____   OTHER SPECIFICS _____

_____

CONFIRMATION # _____   BY _____   DATE _____

PRICES _____ per person ____ air/sea ____ cruise only

Port taxes _____ other charges _____

TOTAL DUE _____   DEPOSIT _____   OPTION DATE _____

FINAL PAYMENT _____   DUE _____

Payment made by ___ cash ___ check ___ credit card: _____

Payment made by ___ cash ___ check ___ credit card: _____

- -

AIR/SEA PACKAGE INCLUDES: _____

FLIGHTS: _____

TICKETS RECEIVED/DONE ____CRUISE ____FLIGHTS   GIVEN TO CLIENT ON_____ DATE

OTHER: ___Bon Voyage Gift:_____

___Travel Bag/Passport wallet ___Travel Checklist, Cruise Information Sheet

___Insurance Waiver/Information Other _____

FOLLOW UP_____   DATE _____

CRUISE RESERVATION/INQUIRY FORM

NAME(S): _____ CITIZENSHIP _____

ADDRESS _____

PHONE(S) home _____ work _____ E-mail_____

NO.OF
ADULTS _____ CHILDREN _____ AGES _____ PREVIOUS CRUISES:_____
_____

DEPARTURE   NO.OF
DATE(S)_____ALTERNATIVES_____DAYS_____
- -

1st CRUISE LINE: _____ SHIP _____
PHONE # _____ SAILING DATE _____
CABIN CATEGORY/TYPE REQUESTED _____
CATEGORY/CABIN CONFIRMED: _____ DECK _____
MEAL SITTING _____ OTHER SPECIFICS _____
_____

CONFIRMATION # _____ BY _____ DATE _____
PRICES _____ per person ____ air/sea ____ cruise only
Port taxes _____ other charges _____
TOTAL DUE _____ DEPOSIT _____ OPTION DATE _____
FINAL PAYMENT _____ DUE _____
Payment made by ___ cash ___ check ___ credit card: _____
Payment made by ___ cash ___ check ___ credit card: _____
- -

2ND CRUISE LINE: _____ SHIP _____
PHONE # _____ SAILING DATE _____
CABIN CATEGORY/TYPE REQUESTED _____
CATEGORY/CABIN CONFIRMED: _____ DECK _____
MEAL SITTING _____ OTHER SPECIFICS _____
_____

CONFIRMATION # _____ BY _____ DATE _____
PRICES _____ per person ____ air/sea ____ cruise only
Port taxes _____ other charges _____
TOTAL DUE _____ DEPOSIT _____ OPTION DATE _____
FINAL PAYMENT _____ DUE _____
Payment made by ___ cash ___ check ___ credit card: _____
Payment made by ___ cash ___ check ___ credit card: _____
- -

AIR/SEA PACKAGE INCLUDES: _____
FLIGHTS: _____
TICKETS RECEIVED/DONE _____CRUISE _____FLIGHTS GIVEN TO CLIENT ON_____ DATE
OTHER: ___Bon Voyage Gift:_____
___Travel Bag/Passport wallet ___Travel Checklist, Cruise Information Sheet
___Insurance Waiver/Information Other _____
FOLLOW UP_____ DATE _____

ROLE-PLAY EVALUATION FORM

STUDENT _____   CLIENT(S) _____

The first evaluation relates to the agent's approach and greeting:

_____Answered phone quickly (second or third ring at least)

_____Used correct phone answering/greeting (identified self, agency)

_____Sounded enthusiastic ("smile in the voice," positive tone)

_____Sounded professional and prepared (no hesitation, organized, ready to take details)

Then, the agent's attitude and voice qualities:

___Sounded pleased	___Sounded nervous	___Sounded bored
___Voice just right	___Voice too loud	___Voice too soft/low
___Good rhythm	___Talked too fast	___Talked too slowly
___Pleasing voice quality	___Monotone	___Too much inflection

Then, the exchange of information:

___Obtained who, what, where, how many

___Asked about type of trips taken previously, likes and dislikes, preferences

___Determined possible choices or first considerations, dates, types of accommodations/cabins, alternatives, other considerations

Key points related to specfic situations:

___Presented specific details and information

___Presented benefits of features

___Used open-ended questions

___Handled objections

___Did (or arranged to do so) pertinent research

___Recognized buying signals

___Offered to make tentative reservations

___Obtained reservations

___Collected deposits/full payments

___Answered all clients' questions

___Made appropriate recommendations

___Closed the call professionally

___Thanked the clients

OTHER COMMENTS _____

_____

_____

Evaluated by _____

CHAPTER 7

Tests, Promotions, and Other Topics

HIGHLIGHTS OF THIS CHAPTER INCLUDE:

- ✦ Tests on Cruise Lines and Ships
- ✦ Marketing and Promotions
- ✦ Selling Cruises to Groups
- ✦ Family Cruises
- ✦ Meetings at Sea
- ✦ Other Topics
- ✦ Spotlight on Carnival Cruise Lines

TESTS ON CRUISE LINES AND SHIPS

CHAPTER 7, TEST 1

Match the following ships with cruise lines. *Note:* Some answers may be used more than once, and some may not be used at all. Information is subject to change.

1._____ *Westerdam*	A. Norwegian Cruise Line
2._____ *Noordam*	B. American Canadian Caribbean
3._____ *Sun Princess*	C. Regal
4._____ *Regal Empress*	D. Cunard
5._____ *Caribbean Prince*	E. Delta Queen Steamboat
6._____ *Norwegian Sky*	F. Princess
7._____ *Mississippi Queen*	G. Crystal
8._____ *Fantasy*	H. Carnival
9._____ *Celebration*	I. Holland America
10._____ *Horizon*	J. Celebrity Cruises
11._____ *Queen Elizabeth 2*	K. Costa Cruises
12._____ *Costa Romantica*	L. Royal Caribbean International
13._____ *Adventure of the Seas*	M. Wind Star Cruises
14._____ *Song of Norway*	N. Bergen Line
15._____ *Wind Star*	O. Clipper Cruises
16._____ *Zenith*	P. Royal Olympic Line
17._____ *Jubilee*	
18._____ *Norwegian Dream*	
19._____ *Sovereign of the Seas*	
20._____ *Millennium*	

CHAPTER 7, TEST 2

1. Name five activities that can be enjoyed on a cruise. _____
_____

2. What particular items help determine the cost of a cruise? _____
_____

3. Name three factors that should be considered in selecting the right cruise for a client. _____
_____

4. What are three advantages of cruises? _____
_____

5. What are three disadvantages? _____
_____

6. In addition to qualifying the client, name three other skills for selling cruises. _____
_____

7. Name the three key points about selling cruises. _____
_____

8. Define guaranteed share rate. _____
_____

9. The direction toward the wind is _____, and the direction away from the

   wind is _____.

10. Give sample times for the early/first sitting for meals on cruises.

   Breakfast_____ Lunch_____ Dinner_____

CHAPTER 7, TEST 3

1. A suggested amount to tip the cabin steward is _____ per person per day.

2. What are stabilizers? _____
_____

3. _____means to go aboard, and _____means to get off the ship.

4. Where you leave and enter the ship is called the _____.

5. Name three ports in Florida for departing on Caribbean cruises. _____
_____

6. What are five other cruising areas of the world besides the Caribbean? _____
_____

7. Name three countries that offer barge cruises. _____
_____

8. The port of Athens, Greece, is _____.

9. Most eastbound transatlantic cruises leave New York and arrive in either _____

   or _____.

10. Embarkation usually begins about _____ to _____ hours before sailing.

11. Name 10 islands that are popular ports of call in the Caribbean. _____

    _____

    _____

12. What are some reasons passengers should book shore excursions through the cruise line? _____

    _____

    _____

13. How can agencies compete with a competitor's discounted cruise prices? _____

    _____

    _____

14. CLIA stands for _____

15. What items should be checked when cruise tickets/documents are received? _____

    _____

16. Why is it important to obtain the citizenship of the clients? _____

    _____

17. Cruises to Bermuda will usually leave from Philadelphia or _____, and they are

    usually seasonal, such as from April to _____.

18. The El Yunque Rain Forest, El Morro, Fort San Cristobal, and the Pablo Casals Museum are

    attractions of the port of _____ on _____ (island).

19. Famous Seven Mile Beach, the Turtle Farm, and the city of Hell are sights on the island of

    _____.

20. The port of Charlotte Amalie and an area of many shops, is on the island of _____.

MARKETING AND PROMOTIONS

Travel agencies should analyze their product mix and redirect business to products such as cruises since they yield higher profits. Determine the most profitable kinds of cruise products for the agency to sell and establish preferred supplier relationships. Take advantage of programs offered by organizations (ASTA, ICTA, CLIA, etc.) and attend conferences that feature ship inspections and cruise travel. Broaden the agency's focus to include niche markets, such as families and special interest groups. Travel agencies can promote cruise sales and increase their profits in a variety of ways:

JOIN A CONSORTIUM—Consortiums or agency groups that focus on cruise sales offer assistance in promotions, better commissions, discount prices, and more.

DESIGNATE AN EMPLOYEE TO BE CRUISE SPECIALIST—Put the employee on an incentive program that pays a $20.00 bonus over his or her salary for every "longer than seven day" cruise sold. As sales increase, a possible commission-only basis might be in order. In designating the specialist, make certain to equip the agent with references, cruise experiences, and thorough training.

ADVERTISING—Feature cruises in an advertisement about your agency. For example, run a small ad in the newspaper for a long time as a tag to a cruise line or just featuring your cruise specialist.

CRUISE NIGHTS—Invite the public/clients to your agency or a hotel for a presentation. Work with cruise lines for brochures, giveaways, videos, and the like. For real innovation, hold the cruise night at a local car dealership or real estate office. In exchange for a mailing list of their customers and the space, allow the company five minutes of presentation time. (See the sample checklist for a successful cruise night.)

CRUISE DAYS—Set up a "Cruise Day" in the cafeteria of a commercial account or business with a brief presentation, video, and so on.

DIRECT MAIL—Mail flyers, letters, or brochures to existing clients or prospects. Work with a select group of clients, adding a personal note to a new brochure or flyer. Introduce a special sailing with a coupon for something like "$10.00 OFF."

STUFFERS—Include a flyer with every airline ticket sold.

RADIO SPOTS—Select an advertisement effective as a radio commercial.

TELEMARKETING CAMPAIGN—Call clients or prospects about an upcoming cruise or special rates in effect.

WINDOW DISPLAY—Feature cruises with nautical items, posters, popular souvenirs, cruise ship models, videos, and the like.

PROMOTE GROUPS ON CRUISES—A section of this chapter is dedicated to group travel and cruises.

Checklist for a Successful Cruise Night

1. Select a cruise night coordinator who will be responsible for most details.

2. Select a date (allowing three to four months' lead time). Avoid conflict with other events. *Note:* Usually midweek about 7:00 P.M. works well for attendance.

3. Compile the guest list. Decide if it will be small or large. Choose experienced cruise clients, clients who have never cruised, commercial account clients, incentive travel groups, or a particular market segment.

4. Select a site and reserve it. Your office may work for a small group. Try school auditoriums, community halls, or hotel meeting rooms for large groups. For innovation, coordinate your cruise night with a company that can provide you with their customer mailing list in exchange for a brief presentation to the attendees. Expect about 50% attendance from your mailing list.

5. Negotiate a special cruise rate, if possible, or decide on a discount that you might be able to offer for immediate reservations.

6. Arrange for catering (simple hors d'oeuvres and punch/wine).

7. Decide on a possible theme or destination and plan decor accordingly. Add special effects, such as a cruise fashion show, coordinated with a local store.

8. Develop the program. Plan the opening and closing events. Decide on music, audio/visual aids, brochures, door prizes, and so on. If you use a video, make it a short one (20 to 30 minutes maximum). Invite local sales representatives from the cruise line(s) you will feature. Remember to give credit to any sponsors and contributors. Avoid the hard sell approach if taking reservations, and emphasize the convenience of booking on site as well as the special price (if applicable).

9. Mail invitations (at least three weeks in advance). Include the date, time, place, and RSVP information. It is best to hand-address and mail first class. Follow up with phone calls to those invited to maximize response. Keep a list of those invited and attendees for future reference (call after the event for possible sales).

10. Publicize the event (press releases to local newspapers, radio, TV, bulletin boards, etc.).

11. Personally inspect the facility at least a week before to handle any possible problems.

12. Prepare the staff and name tags, inspect the facility, check on all the items. Outline the program and brief the staff on the specifics.

13. Be there at least 30 to 45 minutes prior and start on time.

14. Send attendees a follow-up thank you.

SELLING CRUISES TO GROUPS

All kinds of groups—families, business associates, employees of a company, school or college reunion groups, hobby groups, church groups, investment clubs, neighborhoods, apartment complexes, sports activity groups—enjoy cruises. Affinity groups (people who have something in common) are more available to travel year-round. Affinity groups are easier to sell because the organization is already there. And the fallout (cancellations) is also lower with affinity groups. The other kind of group available is a "speculative" group, because the agency has to advertise, promote, and sell a number of passengers who don't necessarily have any connection with each other.

The group sales department of the cruise line can help in providing the extras that make the cruise truly special. Fundraisers generate cruise groups. You can raffle off the free tour conductor's cabin and use the proceeds for a charity or donate a portion of each group member's cruise fare to a worthy cause. Careful planning is in order, as groups take at least nine to 12 months' lead time to put together.

Sample Group Sales Policies of Cruise Lines

Note: They are subject to change.

DISNEY CRUISE LINE—One tour conductor free for every 16 passengers (8 cabins). Discounts slightly higher than early booking discounts.

DELTA QUEEN STEAMBOAT—One free for the first 10 full-fare passengers, 2 for 30 passengers, 3 for 40, and 4 for 50. Discounts 10% to 50% on yield management basis. Also, free or reduced air.

HOLLAND AMERICA—Tour conductor free with 15 paid passengers.

NORWEGIAN CRUISE LINE—One free for every 15 fare paid passengers.

ORIENT LINES—One free for every 15 paid passengers.

PRINCESS—One for every 9 passengers for cruises over 7 days, one for every 15 passengers on cruises of 7 days.

RADISSON—One for every 10 full-fare adult passengers.

REGAL CRUISES—One for every 15 passengers.

ROYAL CARIBBEAN INTERNATIONAL— One for every 16 passengers.

SEABOURN—One for every 5 full-fare suites.

SILVERSEA—One for every 9 full-fare passengers.

STAR CLIPPERS—One for every 10 passengers.

WINDSTAR—One for every 10 passengers.

When working with the groups sales department of the cruise line, here are some of the extras that may be negotiated:

- Cooperative advertising, such as shared mailing costs, a group cruise brochure, and so on.
- An hour-long cocktail party the evening of departure
- $50.00 shipboard credit for the first X number of cabins
- A shore excursion to the group at no cost
- Complimentary group photograph

FAMILY CRUISES

All ships are not alike in what they offer for children and teens traveling with adult members. Agents booking families should check cabin size and facilities before booking four people to a stateroom. A family may be better off booking two cabins or a suite. Most children's programs on cruise ships are free, although some charges are made for tours or special activities. Check to be sure the program is available, what hours it encompasses, and other specifics. Here's a list of some cruise lines and their activities and facilities for children and teens:

CARNIVAL CRUISE LINES carries more than a quarter of a million kids a year, and its Camp Carnival program is very attractive. The line features spacious cabins (many offering accommodations up to five people), as well as adjoining cabins. Activities are organized for toddlers (2 to 4) to teens (13 to 16). Karaoke parties, photography and art classes are some of possibilities.

CELEBRITY CRUISES—Supervised programs for children age 3 to 17 are available—divided into four age groups. The line has eight counselors on each ship during holidays and school vacation periods.

COSTA CRUISES has supervised activity programs for children 3 years old and older on Caribbean and European sailings. On "Parents Night Out," the kids are fed and looked after the entire evening.

CRYSTAL CRUISES offers a program for three different age groups during holiday cruises and selected summer sailings. There are no four-berth cabins, but some suites can accommodate families.

CUNARD LINE's *Queen Elizabeth 2* has a nanny-supervised program with separate facilities for infants to teens. On transatlantic crossings, families can even bring the dog along—there's a kennel topside.

DISNEY CRUISE LINE's supervised programs are available from 9 A.M. to midnight for children age 3 to 8 and 9 to 12 years. Group babysitting for children age 12 weeks to 3 years old is $6.00 per child an hour and $5.00 per hour for each additional child.

HOLLAND AMERICA LINE offers supervised programs for the age 4 to 17 cruiser. The line offers several naturalist and learning programs.

NORWEGIAN CRUISE LINE has a Kids Crew program designed for those age 3 to 17. Teens have their own space with discos and games. Special activities are planned for each age group during stops at NCL's private island in the Bahamas.

PRINCESS CRUISES offers the Love Boat Kids Programs with a minimum age of 2 and a teen program extended to 16-year-olds. Programs are available year-round on newer ships and seasonally when there are 15 or more children in applicable age groups on board.

ROYAL CARIBBEAN INTERNATIONAL's Aquanauts Program is for those age 3 to 5, Explorers is for age 6 to 8, Voyagers for those age 9 to 12, and Navigators for age 13 to 17. Activities for younger children operate until 10 P.M. while those for teens extend until 1 A.M. and the program is available year-round on all the ships. Adventure and learning are emphasized.

WINDJAMMER BAREFOOT CRUISES offers Junior Jammers Kids Club in summer months aboard the *Legacy* and *Polynesia*. The active program for children age 6 to 12 stresses learning and nature.

MEETINGS AT SEA

More and more ships are enhancing their business amenities, which makes for more inviting meetings at sea. Advantages of meetings on a cruise include:

- The audience is captive—passengers can't very well get off the ship while sailing.
- Price is attractive—especially considering what the cruise rate includes.
- Family travel can be accommodated along with the business agenda—no need for the meeting planner to arrange spouse and guest activities.

WHEN PLANNING FOR A GROUP MEETING ON BOARD, DETERMINE FROM THE GROUP:

- Is the size of the group large enough to command a complete charter of the ship?
- What size meeting space is required?
- A/V equipment and visuals needed
- Other technical equipment necessary
- Any special needs for passengers
- Is the itinerary satisfactory?
- Who will be billed for the charges?

WHEN WORKING WITH THE CRUISE LINE FOR THE MEETING, FIND OUT:

- Is A/V and tech support available on the ship?

- Confirm all specifics: dates, rates, amenities, types of cabins, meeting space, dining arrangements, liquor policies, room gifts, organized activities/events, pre-arranged shore excursions, changes in prices if there is a change in number, payment policies, cancellation policies, and all other particulars

- Are round-trip transfers from the airport to the port provided?

- What ground operators are involved for any group shore excursions?

The meeting planner should be personally familiar with the ship. Confirm all arrangements when booked, when paid, and again before the departure. Confirm passenger names with cruise line at the time of deadline (usually 60 days prior). Use organized lists for all the steps involved (handbooks on meeting planning assist you with all details).

OTHER TOPICS

CRUISE-ONLY TRAVEL AGENCIES—There are a growing number of cruise-only travel agencies, which may not have the Airlines Reporting Corporation (ARC) approval that allows them to issue airline tickets. Cruise-only agencies specialize in cruises, but in some cases will sell tours and other travel products. An alliance may be formed with a travel agency who issues the airline tickets needed, and the two agencies "split" the commission. Cruise consortiums, franchisers, and organizations can be of great assistance.

INCREASED CRUISE COMMISSIONS—Overrides or increased commissions are available to agencies that belong to a consortium, chain, franchiser, or other association/organization. Overrides or bonuses may also be available based on the volume of sales with specific cruise lines. Contact the agency groups as well as the individual cruise lines to find out their bonus/increased commission programs. *The Travel Dictionary* and other trade references list consortiums/organizations.

CRUISE SPECIALISTS—Many agencies employ cruise specialists or designate an area of the agency for featuring cruise products and sales. Since cruises are popular and earn higher commissions than airline tickets, it's a good idea for all agents to be knowledgeable about cruises. A library of references, an incentive program (rewarding agents who reach goals in sales), and an ongoing training program should be used. Agents should attend conferences, trade shows, and ship inspections that are offered throughout the year. These are generally advertised in travel industry publications.

GETTING A JOB WITH A CRUISE LINE—Many people dream of getting a job with a cruise line. Contact the various lines for information. *The Travel Industry Personnel Directory* is extensive for company listings. *How to Get a Job with a Cruise Line* provides insiders' tips to the jobs on board the ships. Contact bookstores to order either of these references.

PASSENGER SERVICES ACT/JONES ACT—Did you ever wonder why you can't take a cruise from one U.S. city to another? The Passenger Services Act of 1886/Jones Act declared that foreign flag vessels taking U.S. passengers must stop at a foreign port before returning those passengers to the United States. Only a few cruise lines sail under the U.S. flag, such as Delta Queen Steamboat Company, and Clipper Cruise Line—allowing them to travel between U.S. ports of call. There have been efforts to change this antiquated law, which obviously favors foreign ports of call. Keep in touch with news sources for possible update.

QUICK REFERENCE CRUISE LINES—WEB SITES

American Canadian Caribbean Line	<http://www.accl-smallships.com>
Carnival Cruise Lines	<http://www.carnival.com>
Celebrity Cruises	<http://www.celebrity-cruises.com>
Clipper Cruise Line	<http://www.clippercruise.com>
Costa Cruises	<http://www.costacruises.com>
Cruise West	<http://www.cruisewest.com>
Crystal Cruises	<http://www.crystalcruises.com>
Cunard	<http://www.cunardline.com>
Delta Queen Steamboat Co.	<http://www.deltaqueen.com>
Disney Cruises	<http://www.disney.com>
Holland America	<http://www.hollandamerica.com>
Norwegian Cruise Line	<http://www.ncl.com>
Orient Lines	<http://www.orientlines.com>
Peter Dielmann Cruises	<http://www.deilmann-cruises.com>
Princess Cruises	<http://www.princesscruises.com>
Radisson Seven Seas Cruises	<http://www.rssc.com>
Regal China Cruises	<http://www.regalchinacruises.com>
Regal Cruises	<http://www.regalcruises.com>
Royal Caribbean Int'l	<http://www.royalcaribbean.com>
Royal Olympic	<http://www.royalolympiccruises.com>
Silversea	<http://www.silversea.com>
Star Cruises	<http://www.starclippers.com>
Victoria Cruises	<http://www.victoriacruises.com>
Windjammer Cruises	<http://www.windjammer.com>
Windstar	<http://www.windstarcruises.com>
World Explorer	<http://www.wecruise.com>

SPOTLIGHT ON CARNIVAL CRUISE LINES

Carnival Cruise Lines is a member of the exclusive World's Leading Cruise Lines alliance, which also includes Holland America Line, Cunard Line, Seabourn Cruise Line, Costa Cruises, and Windstar Cruises. Together, these member lines share a commitment to quality cruise vacations, that appeal to a wide range of lifestyles, budgets, and interests. Carnival is a leader in the contemporary cruise marketplace.

Carnival Cruise Line began with pioneer Ted Arison, who set out to make a vacation experience once reserved for the very rich accessible to the average traveler. Here is a brief history of this cruise line and its accomplishments:

1972—Maiden voyage of Carnival's first ship, the *Mardi Gras,* which runs aground on a sandbar off the Coast of Miami.

1975—Carnival purchases the *Empress of Britain* and renames her the *Carnivale.*

1978—Carnival begins service on the *Festivale,* formerly the *S.A. Vaal,* which becomes the fastest and largest vessel sailing from Miami to the Caribbean.

1982—The *Tropicale* debuts as the first new cruise ship, marking the beginning of an industry-wide multibillion-dollar boom in ship building.

1984—Carnival is the first cruise line to advertise on TV, with the premiere of ads featuring Kathie Lee Gifford (then Johnson).

1985—The 46,052-ton *Holiday* begins service.

1986—The 47,262-ton *Jubilee* debuts.

1987—The *Celebration,* also 47,262 tons, debuts. Carnival earns the distinction of being the "most popular cruise line in the world," as it carries more passengers than any other.

1990—The 70,367-ton *Fantasy* enters service and is the first of the "Fantasy-class" vessels. Eventually, Carnival constructs eight "Fantasy-class" ships, the most ships in a single class.

1991—The 70,367-ton *Ecstasy* begins service.

1993—A third 70,367-ton ship, the *Sensation,* debuts.

1995—The *Imagination,* again 70,367 tons, begins its service.

1996—The sixth "Fantasy-class" ship called the *Inspiration* starts sailing.

Carnival debuts the first passenger vessel to exceed 100,000 tons, the *Carnival Destiny* (101,353 tons).

1998—The *Elation,* the seventh "Fantasy-class" ship emerges.

The eighth and last in the "Fantasy-class" of ships begins service—the *Paradise,* which sails as the world's first totally "smoke-free" cruise ship.

1999—The 102,000-ton *Carnival Triumph,* the second "Destiny-class" vessel, starts service.

2000—The 102,000-ton *Carnival Victory* (third "Destiny-class" ship), debuts.

2001—Carnival introduces the "Spirit-class" vessels, with the launch of the 88,500-ton *Carnival Spirit.* This is the first new "Fun Ship" ever positioned in the Alaska and Hawaii markets. The *Tropicale* is transferred to Costa Cruises.

2002—Two more "Spirit-class" ships, the *Carnival Pride* and *Carnival Legend.* Also, the 110,000-ton *Carnival Conquest,* a larger, longer version of the "Destiny-class" ships, debuts.

2003—The *Carnival Glory,* a second 110,000-ton ship.

2004—The *Carnival Miracle,* the fourth in the "Spirit-class" category, is scheduled to enter service in 2004

The *Carnival Valor,* a third 110,000-ton ship is expected to debut, bringing the total number of ships in the fleet to 21!

Index